CONTENTS

INTRODUCTION

Although I have been studying and teaching the martial arts for more than 30 years, I am still amazed at how much there is to learn. In fact, the expansiveness of the fighting arts is one of the wonderful aspects about them that keeps so many talented, creative, and curious people involved year after year.

Although *Power Training* can stand by itself, I see it closely linked to *Speed Training*, also published by Paladin Press. When I first began working on *Speed Training*, the idea of a follow-up book on developing power was the furthest thing from my mind. I was interested only in learning about speed: how to develop it, how to keep it, how to teach it to others, and how best to pass on my learning in book form to people I had never met. As I said in *Speed Training*, I have always been fascinated with speed and feel fortunate to have seen and trained with some incredibly fast fighters.

I have never given much thought to power since I have been blessed with good natural strength and have developed additional strength over the years as a result of regular training with weight-resistance exercises. But until recently, weight training was only an activity I did in addition to my martial arts training. I never lifted specifically to enhance my martial arts but as a separate objective for fitness and appearance sake.

But during the course of conducting research for *Speed Training*, I found lots of information on developing powerful kicks, punches, blocks, and throws. In fact, I found that some of the same exercises used to develop speed can be used to develop power.

Are not fast hands and fast feet enough? There are a lot of martial art systems and individual fighters who believe they are. But ask yourself this: would you rather be struck once by a 240-pound fighter who is slow and sluggish or a fighter who weighs 135 pounds and can hit three times in the same amount of time it takes the big guy to hit once?

Before you answer that, consider these possibilities. What if that 240-pound fighter has developed great speed and power and has learned how to apply both in his techniques? Or what if that 135-pound fighter has trained to hit lightning fast and, as a result of using specific power exercises, is able to hit as hard as a heavyweight? Are these realistic possibilities? Yes. Can you achieve these objectives? Absolutely.

In the course of researching *Speed Training*, I learned that speed is much more complex than simply moving fast. Likewise, in researching this book, I learned that there is much more to power than just strength. Just because a fighter possesses big muscles doesn't mean he can punch hard. There are many bulky bodybuilders around who are unable to transfer all their muscle and strength into practical application, particularly fighting techniques.

There have been many occasions when I have experienced power that surprised me. One time I was teaching the telescopic police baton to a class of police officers. At one point I was dressed in the "Red Man" suit, a red, thickly padded outfit consisting of a helmet and large wraparound foam rubber sections that protect the chest, back, groin, and legs. My job was to advance on each officer as he practiced sidestepping, shuffling, striking, and thrusting.

There were three big guys in the class, big like the cops they used to hire in the old days. I found that I could easily sidestep these guys and sometimes give them a nudge to send them flying. When they did land a solid blow, I occasionally felt its sting through the thick padding.

But it was a guy who stood 5 feet 6 inches, tipped the scales at about 130, and had trained in the martial arts who stopped me in my tracks. In fact, he was the only person able to hurt me through that heavily padded suit. Although he was not muscular, it was obvious that he was in shape, and it was apparent that he knew how to use correct body mechanics to bring out exceptional power from his slight body. His swings at my legs sent shock waves all the way through my bones, and his thrust to my midsection made me feel as if I hadn't any protective gear on at all.

I have been hurt by other people of small stature, fighters who obviously had trained to deliver their techniques with power as well as speed. I have also been hit by big guys who have trained to transfer their strength and weight into devastating blows. The point here is that since physical size isn't always an indicator of power, you should never underestimate a small person. Bruce Lee weighed less than 140 pounds but could punch and kick like a man weighing twice that much (more on this later).

This book examines all facets of power and the many ways to develop it. Unlike speed training where the majority of exercises necessitate a training partner, developing power mostly involves training by yourself. The effort is all yours, but then so are the rewards.

Your goal in developing power for the martial arts is not to be able to lift heavy weights only so that you can lift heavy weights. Of course, your ability to lift heavy objects will increase, but your primary objective is to develop greater power in your blocks, punches, kicks, and throws.

A nice side benefit of training for power is that you will improve your appearance. Weight training, free-hand exercises, specific martial art drills, and good eating habits will forge your frame into a hard body. Depending on how you train and your genetics, you may increase the size of your muscles, or you may just tone what you already have. This is not a bad deal: you will look better, and you will hit harder too. Two for the price of one.

The book begins with a brief look at ki power and examines the age-old question of whether such power really exists. It's known that there are many charlatans around who attempt to pass themselves off as masters of ki, and we also know there are masters who quietly display a strange force that is virtually beyond comprehension.

There is a chapter that looks at several long-established styles recognized for specific techniques that are especially powerful or that have unique ways of developing explosive power. Along the same line, we will examine exercises from the past, some of them hundreds of years old, to find out whether they are still of value today.

Then we will take a big look at the many forms of resistance exercises, such as free weights, dynamic tension, free hand, and plyometrics. Although there are many other exercises in existence, the ones discussed and illustrated here are limited to just those applicable to martial artists.

Throughout this book, you will see how the proper use of body mechanics, especially hip rotation, can increase power, sometimes even doubling it. You will learn how to increase flexibility in your kicks and how to put power in your stretched muscles to kick harder.

Can you deliver awesome power when punching from only one inch away from the target? Yes, and from this book you will learn how to do it much the same as Bruce Lee did it years ago.

Just in case your future opponent reads this book before you do, you will be given some ideas as to how to defend against a fighter who possesses great power.

Completely free of charge, I have included a trouble-shooter quick list that addresses typical problems about power development. And at the end of the book, you will find a section called "Bits of Wisdom," short items of advice to help you develop and release all the power of which you are capable.

FREE TIP FOR THOSE OVER 30

When I passed the big Three-Oh 20 years ago, I began to think and worry about how long I would hold onto my speed and power and whether I could even progress any further in them.

I'm here to tell you this: don't sweat it. You have got many years of progress in front of you. Today, men and women in all athletic endeavors are blowing away the long-held theories about age sapping the strength, speed, and skill of the over-30 athlete. How are they fighting it? By training consistently.

Far too many athletes hang up their athletic supporters and sport bras when they reach some magical age when they think they can no longer make progress. Unfortunately, it's seldom because of physical reasons but, rather, a result of listening to that little voice in their heads. When their minds tell them they will no longer progress, they won't.

Another element that inhibits the aging athlete is a lack of motivation to push, to compete, to continue seeking what he or she is capable of. I was 45 when I stopped competing in karate tournaments, not because of motivational problems but as a result of injuries. But, admittedly, that burning drive was starting to cool for me. It was getting harder and harder to train for that competitive edge because I was having trouble convincing myself that it was still important to continue winning those gaudy plastic trophies.

Lack of time is another element that convinces the over-30 athlete to pack it in. In my unasked-for opinion, this is the poorest excuse of all. Although lack of time can be a problem, it's one that can be managed. I have noticed that people who say they don't have time to train somehow find time to drink beer with their co-workers, coach Little League, tinker in the garage in the evenings, and watch three games on the tube over the weekend. Granted these enjoyable activities are all part of life, especially grown-up life. But they are nonetheless time slots that can be divided, shared, parceled, or in some way managed so that training time can be inserted.

According to Dr. William Evans, director of Pennsylvania State University's Noll Laboratory for Human Performance, the factors that make young athletes successful are the same ones that positively affect the performance of master athletes. "It is consistency of training that determines the extent to which you will excel in sports at an older age. You have to find a way to put in the time."

A sense of impending physical deterioration slows some people. It's true that after the age of 30, a person loses about six to seven pounds of muscle every decade. But only if nothing is done about it. A 10-year study at the University of Florida showed that people who did only aerobic activity, such as running, shadow boxing, and sparring, lost muscle mass at this same rate. But those who practiced aerobics and resistance exercise, such as weight training, maintained their muscle mass.

I was surprised while working on *Speed Training*, as well as on this book, to find that I had progressed in both areas, sometimes rapidly. I experimented with the many exercises, drills, and concepts in both books. Some I liked, some I didn't (though I included the ones I didn't like in the books, anyway, in case others might like them), and some I avoided because they endangered old injuries.

The exercises in which I made the most progress were the ones I did with the most consistency. For example, I practiced one of the kicking drills illustrated in this book three days a week for eight weeks. At the end of that period, my basic kicks had become crisper and faster and had developed so much power that my bag holders complained. At the same time, I practiced lateral raises using dumbbells to work my shoulders, following a concept in this book called "speed reps," an exercise in which you do as many reps as you can in a minute. At the end of only three weeks, I had increased the poundage by 50 percent and the number of reps by 15. My new power was noticeable in the speed and explosiveness of my backfist. Not bad for a guy with gray hair.

The decision is yours, old-timer. But I guarantee that if you use the hard-earned wisdom of your age to put together a training regimen from the many methods illustrated in this book, you will amaze yourself and your friends and enjoy many more years of training.

OK, enough chitchat. You won't get strong unless you get going.

CHAPTER ONE

KI POWER

Over the years I have heard and read many fantastic stories about ki power. Some of them were clearly flights of fancy, charming Asian myths, or just plain lies. But I have also heard stories from friends, trusted peers in the martial arts, who have witnessed events so startling that months later they were still moved by the experience.

A friend, who has been training in the martial arts for more than 35 years and teaching for at least 30, makes frequent trips to Asia, where he trains in the mountains with his master. He has seen many unusual demonstrations of ki power there, but there was one experience especially unsettling to him.

One day, while he was training outdoors near a village, a rather nondescript fighter appeared and walked over to a high brick wall. The man stood motionless for a moment, then made a short run toward it, leaping high into the air at the last moment, snapping out a perfect sidekick. No, he didn't kick the wall down. That would have been impressive, but it could be argued that the wall was weak and about to fall anyway. What my friend described cannot be explained away so easily.

When the man's leap had reached its highest elevation, he stayed there—freeze frame. Looking like a giant nail in a wall, the man's body remained horizontal to the ground, his foot appearing to be stuck against the bricks. One second went by, and another, and another, then finally he dropped back to the ground. Was this ki?

Another friend of mine witnessed a demonstration of ki power in Seattle, Washington, several years ago. The master set a half-dozen clay flower pots across the edge of a table top about 12 inches apart and assumed a punching position in front of them. Then in rapid succession, he broke each one with a mighty punch—with blows that never hit the pots, but stopped an inch short of them. Was this ki?

When most veteran martial artists think of ki power, the name Morihei Uyeshiba, founder and master of aikido, immediately comes to mind. His demonstrations of ki were said by observers to be too unbelievable to be real. Even when he was an old man with a flowing white beard, Uyeshiba could toss four highly skilled black belts through the air as if they were children.

On one occasion, so fantastic was his demonstration that many people were convinced the young black belts, out of reverence for the master, allowed him to throw them. But other people, including the black belts who were thrown, said that not only was it real, but that he threw them with a power they could not describe.

WHAT IS KI?

There are many definitions of ki, so many that it would

take several pages to list them all. But we don't need to get into all that for our purposes here. Let's keep it simple and specific to the issue of power.

The Japanese call it *ki*, the Chinese call it *chi*, the Koreans *ja-ryouk* or *cha-ryouk*; in the West it's sometimes called *adrenaline* or *energy*. All of these terms refer to life force, the force that gives a person superhuman strength in an emergency. By whatever name it's called, men the world over have searched for it, fantasized about it, and claimed that they had obtained it. It's believed by some that when a person is in control of ki, he will possess five elements of power:

- Increased physical strength
- The ability to make the body hard
- The ability to make the body light
- The ability to make the body heavy
- The ability to make the body impervious to pain

Let's consider energy for a moment. According to physics, solids, liquids, and gases are composed of vibrating particles of energy, acting and reacting with each other, creating and destroying one another in a world thousands of times smaller than the atom. It's the energy particles and the space in which they live that form and shape a solid or a substance.

Some people believe that ki moves in and throughout all living things, while others believe it has an additional feature that allows it to condense into visible forms of material objects and then dissolve back into its original invisible state. According to some people, a person can control this energy with his mind by using various breathing exercises.

But there are some Japanese aikido masters, considered mavericks in their country as well as here, who say there is too much made of ki power. They say that when an attacker throws a half-hearted, prearranged strike and the defender reacts using a prearranged defense he has practiced many hundreds of times, the result is an effortless technique that looks almost mystical in its flow. The uninitiated are then led to believe that the defender is using the mysterious force of ki.

One master said that great technique is a product of "practice, practice, and more practice," not the application of strange mental powers. But such statements are too pragmatic for some people. They would rather search a lifetime for a power that may or may not exist.

Where there are people who want something badly, there are other people who are more than willing to give it to them. They are the deceivers. They are like the charlatans who rode around the Old West in gaudily painted covered wagons selling bottled tonic that was supposed to be good for "everything that ails you," from balding to warts to tuberculosis. Today, these fakers pretend to possess ki power and put on "demonstrations" to deceive others, perhaps even themselves.

FAKING KI

If you have been training for a few years, you have probably witnessed demonstrations of ki power, such as the following:

- Arrows pressed against the throat
- Catching a bullet in the teeth
- Breaking a concrete slab on a man's chest
- A sword-wielding, blindfolded man slicing a cucumber on a man's (a dumb man's) throat
- The unmovable man
- The unbendable arm

In the 35 years the martial arts have been proliferating in the United States, the power of ki has been given supernatural and religious connotations by charlatans. What better way to recruit students than for a fake to cause a crowd to go "oooh!" and make them think he has reached a level in the martial arts beyond the physical realm.

It's possible that some of the mysticism surrounding the ki is a result of the spiritual orientation of some of the early Asian masters. For example, aikido's founder, Morihei Uyeshiba, was a deeply religious man, and his students may have attributed his incredible skill to his beliefs.

Another factor contributing to ki's mysticism is that some martial art instructors lack experience in and knowledge of their art. Because of their inability to teach physical technique properly or to recognize and correct a student's incorrect application, some instructors take the easy way out and inform the student that the problem lies with his lack of ki.

When mastered, aikido movements can take on the appearance of supernatural strength. When you attack an aikido expert, you will find yourself doing a cartwheel through the air. This is because the expert has trained for years coordinating his mind and body to flow with your force and redirect it into a technique. Ki is involved, as I shall discuss later in this section, but it does not have one thing to do with supernatural ability.

Let's take a look at three examples of fake ki power that are commonly seen at exhibitions. These may appear to be demonstrations of wondrous power to the uninformed, but in reality the techniques work because of the demonstrator's body alignment.

Just Try to Push Over the Master

In this trick, the "expert" assumes a seated position on the floor, knees up, feet spread and flat. The challenger stands to the front, places his hands on the expert's shoulders, and, as instructed, tries to push the expert over. But he can't. He strains, he grunts, he digs in, but the expert is unmovable.

Usually at this point, the expert, or someone on a microphone, tells the onlookers that it's ki power. No way.

To do the trick, the expert must place his palms under

From a seated position, simply press upward against the pusher's elbows so that his energy is directed down, making your seated position more stable.

the challenger's arms at about his elbows and push upward. Because the expert doesn't have to push very hard, the challenger probably won't even notice unless he is part of the trick. The expert must push the challenger's arms upward to a point where the challenger's energy is redirected at a downward angle. His arms don't have to be angled straight down; in fact, the trick works even when his arms are at 45 degrees. From this angle, the push is actually making the expert stronger and more stable in his seated position.

If the pusher is not part of the demonstration, he will be amazed, and the uninformed audience will be awestruck at the expert's incredible ki force. And no doubt the expert will get a few new students, too.

The Unbendable Supported Arm

Some people catch on to this trick right away, and others never see it. Here, the expert places his wrist on a challenger's shoulder, bends his arm a little, and adjusts his feet into a natural position. He tells the sucker, er, the challenger, to try to bend his (the expert's) arm, using whatever grip or position he wants as he pulls with all the force he

Place your arm on the student's shoulder and ask him to bend it. It doesn't matter how hard he tries because all the stress goes onto his shoulder.

can muster. If the expert has a flair for the dramatic, he will pause for a moment, close his eyes, and take a couple of deep breaths as he gathers his super ki. Then, upon the expert's command, the challenger uses one or both of his hands to bend the arm, which of course he can't do.

There have been a couple of occasions when I have performed this trick as a gag. On one occasion, as the challenger struggled to bend my arm, I had a 10-year-old child jump up and drape himself across my ki-saturated biceps.

If you haven't already figured out the trick here, you should be embarrassed. It doesn't matter whether the challenger uses one or two arms or whether three children hang from the master's arm, because all the force being exerted is going into the challenger's shoulder.

On one occasion, the guy trying to bend my arm complained afterward of a sore shoulder—yet he still didn't figure it out.

Ki power? No way.

Breaking Demonstrations

Breaking bricks, boards, and rocks is as old as the martial arts and often synonymous with karate in the minds of the uninformed. Is it because there are so many uninformed people that there are so many fraudulent breaking demonstrations? Maybe, but then fraudulent breaking is often carried out successfully before audiences of experienced martial artists, too.

Martial artists fake breaks for the same reasons they fake rank, titles (incidentally, have you ever looked up karate in the yellow pages in any American city and noticed how many "world champions" there are operating schools?), and tournament wins. Indeed, there are all kinds of scams going on in the martial arts world. Charlatans do it to appear successful, get accolades, respect, money, and students.

Here is how to spot the fake breakers.

Breaking Hand-Held Bricks

With this trick, the breaker holds the ends of two bricks in one hand in such a way that there is a half-inch to a full inch space between them at the top. The expert holds the bricks out with one hand and chops them in half with the other, a feat that looks impressive and brings a chorus of "oohs" from the crowd and starry-eyed looks from the opposite sex.

But it's sleight of hand. By holding the two bricks so that there is a space between them, the first brick strikes the second brick with enough force to break them both. If

Although this demonstration of power looks impressive, the break occurs because the bricks slap together.

the performer tells you the bricks were destroyed by virtue of his ki power, ask him to break just one in the same manner and then watch him squirm his way out of it.

Breaking a Single Brick

In this setup, a brick is placed on a support so that it extends about halfway over the edge. Except for the end that appears to be held by the breaker's hand, the brick is angled slightly off the support. Actually, the holding hand is cupping the end of the brick and angling the extended end slightly upward. When the breaker's other hand chops at the extended end, the hand holding the brick releases it and the brick slams into the support, breaking the brick.

Ki power? No way.

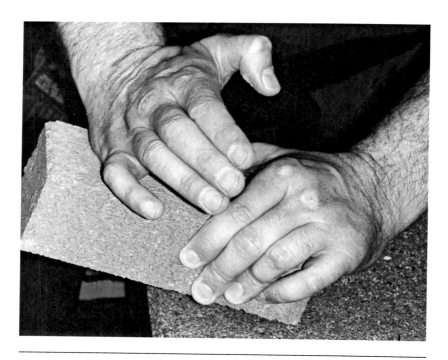

Angling the brick upward from the table's edge will help a blow to slam the brick down and easily break it in half.

Breaking Blocks of Ice

A legitimate ice breaker will stack blocks of ice on top of each other without using spacers to separate them. But how many times have you ever seen that done? The function of the spacer is to create momentum so that the top block breaks the second block, and that one breaks the next, and so on. The bigger the spacer, the easier the break. If the breaker says this isn't so, ask him to break the blocks without them.

This is neither ki power nor muscle power. It's just plain trickery.

Think about this for a moment. If a person is crooked enough to fake breaking techniques, what else is he lying about? Belt rank? Certifications? Tournament wins? Education?

The Death Touch

There are many old stories of the delayed death touch, commonly called dim-mak. The stories usually take place in old Japan or China and involve a highway bandit who makes the grave error of choosing an elderly peasant to rob. But the old man is actually a martial arts master, versed in the death touch. In the process of being robbed, the old master casually touches the bandit on the chest.

The bandit immediately becomes ill and goes to see a doctor. The doctor informs him that he had robbed the village martial arts master. "You will die slowly and painfully," the doctor says. "You have been given the Touch of Death."

Sometimes the bandit dies in the story. Other times he gets well, becomes repentant, and begins a lifelong study under the master.

Is There Such a Thing?

We are far more sophisticated today in the martial arts than we were 20 years ago. Most people no longer think of martial artists as superbeings who can leap atop buildings and run across the surface of a lake, as was often depicted in early martial arts movies. Now, martial artists are generally viewed as athletes with special skills developed from years of diligent training.

The death touch, however, remains in the minds of many fighters—beginners and advanced—as a valid phenomenon. In fact, there are still people who believe that Bruce Lee was killed by the death touch because he offended so many Chinese masters.

Let's take a brief look at the death touch and see whether there are any possible explanations for it.

Poison Hand

This is probably the best explanation I have been able to find. Along with the development of the destructive force of karate and kung fu, many of the old masters were highly skilled in the use of poisons. Some modern-day masters say that in days of old fighters would apply poisons to their hands before touching a victim. The master had to first coat his own hands with some kind of a protective substance so that the poison would not affect him, then put the poison over the protection, go touch his victim, and dash off to wash his hands.

If the victim was not suspicious or had no other reason to bathe, the poison would begin to work through his skin and into his system. Since the passing of poison into the body through the skin is a slow process, the poison's effect was delayed, thereby creating an aura of mystery among the uninformed and uneducated of the day.

Such poisons do exist. In fact, many are undetectable even to today's modern detection methods.

Ki power? Nope.

Psychosomatic Effect

The mind is a powerful instrument and capable of incredible things. There have been cases reported of men being condemned to hang who woke up the morning of their execution to find that they had psychosomatically inflicted rope burns on their necks.

Some people argue that faith healing is all psychosomatic, and so are curses, jinxes, and so on. And it's a good argument. In fact, it's conceivable that a person could actually will himself to die if he was convinced that a master's touch had the ability to inflict death.

Acupuncture/Acupressure

Is there a relationship between the healing arts of acupuncture and the death touch? Some people think there is. If a needle or direct pressure can cause pain and pleasure, and bring pain relief, is it possible that a touch or a blow to an acupuncture point can bring illness or death? Yes. In fact, it was common in the olden days for the village kung-fu master to serve as an instructor in the fighting arts while at the same time acting as the village healer. A person with extensive knowledge in both fields, acupressure in particular, could develop a blow that could be construed as a death touch. One acupressurist/martial artist I interviewed talked of healing points that could be struck to effect major dysfunctions in the body.

It's quite possible that while ki power was and is faked by the unscrupulous, some fighters in old Japan and China used poisons, acupressure, and psychosomatic techniques as legitimate weapons. The uneducated, however, saw them as supernatural forces, so the old masters just grinned and went along with it.

Let's move on from fake ki and take a brief look at what ki really is and how it can help your martial arts.

DEVELOPING KI

I believe that ki is energy, and I will be using both words

interchangeably for the rest of this chapter. There is nothing particularly supernatural, eerie, or mystical about energy, although there are times when a martial artist has so mastered a technique that it looks like it might be. Granted, there are tales of demonstrations, such as those I related at the beginning of this chapter, that have no easy explanation. Of course, stories get changed in the telling, with important elements getting left out, and some get exaggerated. But if those incidents are true, they are so singular and so rare that they are beyond the scope of this book.

Mind-boggling stories aside, you are still left with energy, yours and your opponent's. Through training you can learn to control, guide, and harness this natural energy to add to the elements that increase your power dramatically. When ki is combined with speed, precision movement, and external strength developed from exercises described throughout this book, your overall fighting power becomes incredible. Not supernatural, just incredible.

For ki to flow and do what you want it to do, you must have a positive attitude toward it. Consider the following elements that must be present before you will experience ki flow in your techniques:

- *A positive mind.* Energy is inhibited in a mind that is negative and full of self-doubt. If you don't think it's going to happen, it isn't.
- *Lots of practice.* When you have performed a technique hundreds or thousands of times, you will develop a strong mind-body connection.
- *Mastery of basic body mechanics, sound balance, good speed, and optimum muscular power.*
- *Perfect timing of your exhalation and mental intention.*

Let's see how these elements work together to form power.

A Positive Mind

I once saw a sign posted in a gymnastic school that read: "Whether you think you can or can't, you're right," meaning that you will perform how you *think* you will perform. So why would anyone training in the martial arts want to say things like "I can't side kick," or "my kata sucks," or "I'm terrible at sparring." When people say these things, even if they are being said in an attempt to be humble, they are literally programming their minds to perform negatively.

On the flip side, when you make positive statements such as "I am good at kata," or "my roundhouse kick is fast and powerful," your ever-listening subconscious mind is going to tell your body to do your kata well and launch your kick with speed and power.

Be and act positive. Even if you are having trouble with a technique, speak of it positively, such as, "My punches are getting stronger. I am hitting harder every workout. My power grows every day." Give yourself positive statements, and your body will follow. Ki will not flow in a body that is being choked by a negative mind.

Practice

A yellow belt is the first colored belt earned in my style, and, although the requirements are extensive, I could teach a new student all the physical requirements in one or two nights. Would the student have any skill in the techniques and be able to defend himself with them? Of course not. After only one or two nights of training, the techniques would just be lumped in the doorway of his mind. It takes at least three or four months of consistent, repetitive training before the techniques are absorbed all the way in, and months, perhaps a year, before they know their way around well enough to become part of the body's and mind's natural reflexes.

There are no shortcuts; only repetitive practice will get you there. A master once said that it takes 300,000 repetitions of a technique before a fighter truly knows and understands it. Every rep is like a swipe of sandpaper smoothing the track, creating a friction-free groove so the body and mind are able to function as one.

Body Mechanics, Balance, Speed, and Muscular Power

In folklore, the old kung-fu master would make a barely perceptible movement and his foolish attacker would be thrown to the ground deader than a doornail. Body mechanics, speed, and power were of no consideration because the master simply relied on his ki to devastate his opponent.

By accepting that ki is energy and nothing supernatural, logic tells us that precise body mechanics must be present for energy to flow unencumbered, that there must be muscular power to launch the energy, and that the energy must be transmitted with speed to create great force.

Will a technique work without these elements present? Can a punch to the jaw still hurt even when sloppily delivered? Yes, but not as much. If a blow or a takedown technique has ample speed and power and the target is positioned just right, an opponent can still be hit hard enough to suffer injury. For example, say you slip on the floor during a fight and as you fall you snap your foot into your opponent's groin, or as you flail your arms around, you inadvertently strike your opponent's nose. Sure, these blows can still hurt even though all the elements are lacking and ki is only mildly involved.

Although a technique still has sufficient zip to inflict injury when the elements are weak, only a perfectly aligned body (amazingly, ancient masters figured this out long before there were such sciences as sports medicine and body mechanics), along with highly developed speed and power, can open the door to let ki flow through the technique.

Perfectly Timed Exhalation and Mental Intention

Ki needs a steady exchange of oxygen. Martial arts instructors would be quite wealthy if they were given a dime for every time they said to their students, "Breathe!" and "Don't hold your breath." Erratic breathing—whether it's caused by hard exercise, fear, or anxiety—prevents the smooth flow of ki. When the rhythm of oxygen exchange gets interrupted, ki dissipates, speed and power suffer, and proper technique goes out the window.

Never hold your breath. Keep breathing no matter how tired or scared you are. If you hold your breath when executing a technique, you will prevent ki flow and never release all the speed and power you are capable of. Inhale as you prepare to strike, and exhale as you strike. Although it's considered better to exhale out your nose when delivering a blow, it's OK to exhale out your partially open, tightened lips if you have a cold or sinus problems. Here is how I do it.

The moment my punch takes off, I begin exhaling. It's a mild exhalation at first; then I blow out harder and harder as my punch gets closer to the target. Roughly one inch away, I contract my abdominal muscles as hard as I can and violently discharge the rest of my air. It's as if a big hand suddenly grabs my waist and squeezes, forcing the air up and out my nose. I also exhale when I block, but I don't tense my abdominals as hard unless I am trying to inflict damage on my opponent's attacking limb. When I follow the block with a counterattack, I take a short inhalation and then exhale violently as just described. When I throw three or four counters in rapid combination, I exhale in spurts, saving air to exhale on each technique.

Kata is a good place to practice your breathing. Examine the moves to determine where you can release a lot of air, where you should release only in spurts, or where you should release a long stream. Strive for subtlety; don't heave and gasp like an old workhorse. Always try to conceal your breathing from your opponent. In a moment we will look at some exercises that will facilitate breath control.

It is imperative that powerful mental intention is linked with your perfectly timed exhalation, because they are tied together so closely. Mental intention is also referred to as spirit, concentration, and in Japanese *kime* (notice that the first two letters are *k-i*).

I have always been a stickler for mental intent with my students in class and when I am judging kata at a tournament. There have been times when I have made kata competitors unhappy because I graded them down. Their technique may have been flawless, but their brains were busy deciding whether they would get fries with their burger after the competition. If mental intention isn't there, you will lose the fight. Period.

Ki will not flow if your mind is not in your technique. Your concentration must be in your fist as it drives forward toward the target. It must think strike; it must think penetrate; it must think destroy. Intention produces ki.

All these elements take time to come together. You may first experience them in your reverse punch, then maybe in your front kick, and then in one particular kata. It will happen in piecemeal fashion over time. Your techniques will be faster, smoother, and more powerful. It's a bit of a tease, letting you experience just a little at a time.

Let's examine further the issue of breathing to see how it helps your ki flow.

More on Breathing

You obviously have some idea of how to breathe or you would be six feet under and certainly not reading this. But as is the case with so many things, there are better ways to do it.

Most people breathe too shallowly, using only the top portion of their lungs. This can cause early fatigue and definitely a reduction of ki flow. It's mandatory that you breathe deeply to bring in fresh oxygen to help calm and revitalize your energy.

Breathe in slowly and deeply through your nose for three seconds. Hold the air in your lungs for another three seconds to allow it to flow throughout your body and saturate your system with energizing oxygen. Slowly exhale the air; then repeat the process a few more times. Take time to enjoy the calming sensation that washes over you.

It's important to breathe in through your nose to provide the most efficient exchange of nutrients and waste products in your muscle cells. Breathing in through your mouth only fills the upper and middle portion of your lungs, reducing the efficiency of your air exchange. But inhaling through your nose fills the upper, middle, and lower portions of your lungs.

Is it easy to change your old way of breathing and adopt this method? No. Will you make a complete changeover from the way you have been breathing for years? Probably not. But if you can learn to use this simple breathing process on an as-needed basis, you will be miles beyond where you were before.

This is an effective device to use when you are winded, frightened, anxious, tired, angry, or depressed. Do it prior to taking a big test in school or before you have to give a presentation at a board meeting. Do it between matches at a tournament or when you think the school bully is headed your way. It's an amazingly easy way to calm yourself, gain control of your faculties, and flush your body with flowing ki.

Here is a slightly modified version that is a favorite of mine. The breathing pattern is the same as above, but there is arm movement that you may find helpful. Stand comfortably with your feet about shoulder-width apart and your arms at your sides. As you begin to slowly inhale, turn your palms up and slowly bring them in front of you and up toward your chest. Time your breathing with the lifting of your arms so that your lungs are full by the time your hands are in front of your pectorals, palms up. Hold the air in for three seconds, slowly extend your arms in front of you as if you were pushing something, and simultaneously exhale out your mouth. Pause for two seconds, then slowly bring your hands back as you breathe deeply in through your nose. Your hands stop in front of your chest, as you again pause for three seconds to allow fresh oxygen to flow through your body. Then, as you slowly exhale the air, let your hands descend to your sides as if you were pushing something downward.

The value of this method and the first one is that it restores your mind and body to a calm and energized place where your ki can flow uninterrupted.

Visualize Ki with Your Air Expulsion

Here is a thinking process that you may find beneficial to linking your ki to your exhalation. For this to work,

Mentally project your ki into the target.

however, remember that correct body alignment, speed, power, and mental intent must also be present.

Say you are throwing a fast, powerful, perfectly aligned reverse punch. An inch from the target, you contract your abdominal muscles, exhale an explosion of air, release a mighty shout, and strike with mentally controlled rage. Now let's add a cherry to the pudding, a squirt of Tabasco Pepper Sauce, that extra element that will make your punch the most powerful you are capable of at this moment in your training.

This time as you punch, mentally project your ki into the target. The projection can take on any form you want. Some fighters see their fist traveling beyond the target; some visualize a ghostlike image smashing through the target and traveling beyond. I think of my ki as a red jet stream shooting out the back of my fist like the stream that follows a launched missile or a screaming jet. Then when my fist hits the target and my breath explodes outward, the stream of visualized ki shoots past my fist and continues into the target well beyond the surface. It's part mental, part physical, part faith that it's going to happen. Woe to any innocent people who may be standing behind my target.

Try it.

THE POWER OF THE SHOUT

Can a blood-curdling shout increase power? Yes.

I used to train with a guy who could shout so loudly it probably could have killed a small deer (although I jest that his shout could probably kill a deer, there are stories of masters in old Japan who were said to be able to kill small animals with their shouts). We called him "King of the Kiai." *Kiai* is the Japanese word for the karate shout; Korean martial artists call it *ki-hap* (notice how both words begin with the letters *k-i*). Even as a regular sparring partner, you knew the King was going to do his shout at least a couple times, but it still scared the tar out of you every time.

I can remember several occasions when his shout brought entire tournaments to a momentary standstill as everyone froze in place, looking around to see what was going on. His opponent was instantly reduced to putty, a perfect opportunity for the King to punch a hole through the guy's chest. And he could punch, too, partly because of his physical power and partly as a result of his incredible shout.

My friend had indeed reached a level with his shout that most people never attain or even attempt.

The shout serves three basic functions:

1. *It is a great device for startling or distracting an attacker.* This "freezes" his aggression for a second or two, just long enough for you to attack him.
2. *It makes the upper body slightly invulnerable to pain.* When the shout is brought up from deep within your lower belly, there is a sudden and intense contraction of the abdominal muscles. Say your block misses a roundhouse kick aimed at your midsection. Just as the kick makes contact, exhale sharply as you shout and simultaneously contract the muscles in your stomach, an action that will harden your upper body and enable you to take the impact.

   This also works to minimize pain against a blow to your arms, back, and legs. Timing is critical, however. It won't work if you kiai before the blow hits or after the blow hits. The kiai must be simultaneous with the impact.
3. *It increases your power.* Consciously or unconsciously, you grunt for extra strength when you lift a weight overhead, when you push a car out of a ditch, and when you get your tired, sore body up from the floor after a long training session. A properly executed kiai is many times more powerful than a grunt. It will give you extra speed, power, and ki flow.

The shout is a blending of your mental, spiritual, and

physical being. This is not as mystical as it may sound. With practice, you can develop the ability to mentally focus these three elements into your intended target. It's a matter of reaching into yourself, bringing them up to the surface, and projecting them outward through your techniques.

Kata is a good place to practice your shout. It's your personal fight, just you and those 10 imaginary guys who want to beat you up. It's a great opportunity to use your creativity to pump yourself up to where you can put all your physical, mental, and spiritual energy into your techniques.

Tell yourself you have only one chance to kill the attacker, one chance to survive. This is not the time for wimpy techniques or moves that look as if you are leading a high school cheerleading squad. You must tell yourself, convince yourself, that you have only this chance, this moment to destroy the enemy. You must *feel* the need to destroy; feel it in your heart and in your soul. It must consume your spirit and your mind. Let it fill your muscles with adrenaline. Your shout is not just a release valve; it's a conduit in which your power, speed, precise technique, mental intention, and ki combine and explode.

Where Does It Come From?

A powerful shout starts in your lower abdomen, a place most martial art systems believe is where ki lies and flows from. This is not the same as a muscular midsection, although a strong abdomen can only benefit you.

To execute the shout, take a deep breath and fill your lungs, especially the lower half. Sharply exhale about 25 to 50 percent of your air and then abruptly stop and contract your stomach muscles as you simultaneously and powerfully release your shout. Some fighters release a hissing sound; others grunt "ugh," "ahhh," or "eeeiii." I favor a shout that sounds something like the word "he" because it helps me sharply contract my abdominal muscles as I expel air. It doesn't matter what you shout as long as the utterance works for you.

Remember this: to get the most out of your shout, you must coordinate your mental intention, your physical action, and the explosive expulsion of air and sound. When you have this perfected, your technique will be far more powerful.

· · ·

To summarize, I believe there are far too many things attributed to ki power. I simply define it as energy, life force, being, and breath, all words that have basically the same meaning. I believe ki works when the mind and the body flow together and are in tune with the present. Crucial elements—optimum body mechanics, speed, power, and mental intent—must exist before ki will flow. Ki is a separate element, but also one that requires other elements to be present. When any one of them is weak or nonexistent, ki is weak or nonexistent.

My advice to you is to not make the issue of ki more complex than it needs to be. We all want super power, and many people want to believe there is a force beyond comprehension out there. Maybe there is, maybe there isn't. But this I know for sure: you will progress much faster if you accept ki as an energy force that flows when technique is properly executed. It is a dynamic contributing factor to that thing we want so desperately—power.

And it can be obtained only one way. Practice.

CHAPTER TWO

STYLES

There is a lot of talk about the differences between hard-style and soft-style fighting arts, and, of course, when there is talk about differences, there is always a debate about which one is best.

Well, we are not going to settle that here. Arguments about style and systems are ridiculous, anyway, because superiority boils down to the individual fighter. But we can take a quick, basic look at the elements that make up hard styles and soft styles and see how their differences and similarities relate to their power.

Many people believe that all Japanese and Korean fighting arts are hard and all Chinese fighting arts are soft. Although this is true for the most part, there are exceptions. For example, the Japanese art of aikido is considered soft, and at least one version of hung gar, a kung-fu style, is considered hard.

As is the case with many aspects of the martial arts, there are a variety of explanations as to what the terms hard and soft mean. At the risk of making a complicated subject simplistic, let's define the terms this way: if the fighting art gets most of its power from the external muscles, it's hard style; if the power comes from internal sources, chi or ki, it's soft style.

HARD STYLE

Fighters from hard-style systems train to develop their external bodies to maximize their muscle development. They supplement their martial arts training with weight-resistance exercises, free-hand exercises, running, body toughening, and abdominal crunches.

They use the external muscles of the upper body and the muscles of the legs to propel their punches and kicks. They are concerned with bringing the maximum number of muscles into a move and then tensing them with force at the moment of impact.

Hard stylists continually strive for speed, knowing that with it comes greater power. They work to make their muscles strong and to make those strong muscles move as fast as possible.

Some hard stylists choose to harden such specific body surfaces as their knuckles, sides of their hands, or the balls of their feet. They pound on various objects with their bodies, and they strike various objects against their bodies. Some even go so far as to strike their shins and knuckles with a hammer to develop hard striking surfaces.

SOFT STYLE

Soft stylists (t'ai chi is the most obvious example) usually don't attempt to build the same kind of muscular body as hard stylists. In fact, some avoid it completely. They do emphasize developing their legs, believing that a strong foundation is most important in their art. For example, many of their forms emphasize low stances, which build leg power, while keeping their upper bodies relaxed and pliable.

As I researched the many different soft-style Chinese fighting systems, I discovered a commonality as to how they deliver such tremendous power. Unlike the visually powerful and seemingly rigid Japanese styles, most kung-fu styles appear to be loose and relaxed, almost soft. But the key word here is *appear*, because in reality kung-fu fighters can break boards and bones just as well as fighters from other fighting systems. Being loose and relaxed is not a bad thing with the kung-fu fighter; in fact, it is where their destructive power begins.

Many kung-fu styles believe that when two fighters clash using only exterior brute force, they are using *say sao*, or "dead hands." This means they are using only the strength of their shoulders, arms, and hands. Although this is still powerful, it's weaker than what is possible when the entire body is brought into play. Say sao can also cause a fighter to overextend his power and lose his balance. As discussed elsewhere in this text, this is usually the result of fear, lack of experience, poor training, or all of the above. In addition, continuously using say sao force can be exhausting because the limbs are held so rigidly.

On a pure physical level, kung-fu stylists in general believe that their power begins with a thrust of their legs and the rotation of their hips and waist. The energy then flows upward through their back, their shoulders, and out their hands. This belief is not only a commonality among most Chinese styles, but among the majority of fighting systems from every Asian country, as well as those from Europe and America.

Soft stylists stress ki (or chi, as the Chinese refer to it) to enhance power in their techniques. They rely on internal force as well as their opponent's momentum and body weight to deliver powerful blows and throws. They avoid force-on-force blocks. Instead, they rely more on precise timing to avoid being struck and then they take advantage of their opponent's position and momentum to deliver counterstrikes.

WHICH IS BETTER?

Followers of soft styles believe their ability to release internal power is more effective than using external muscle. Hard stylists believe that soft stylists cannot possibly generate the same kind of power that they can with their highly developed muscles. Although there have been tests conducted to determine which style is stronger, the results have been inconclusive.

I believe in both approaches. I have been around long enough to see that both are valid and capable of delivering tremendous power. I have seen incredible demonstrations of internal power (discarding those that were fake), and I have been the recipient of soft-style blows that knocked me on my behind. I have also seen amazing demonstrations of hard-style power, and I have been on the receiving end of painful blows from them as well.

My approach has been primarily hard style, although I have drawn upon certain elements of soft style. A soft stylist would probably argue that to be a student of internal power, you have to commit 100 percent of your efforts in that direction. This is probably true. However, I have found that some elements of soft style can be adapted without years of dedication.

For example, many of the blocks I teach are soft-style types in that the force is redirected rather than smashed aside. I teach students to evade force whenever possible and to counterattack by using the best technique based on their body position in relation to their opponent's.

I also believe in "thinking" power through a target. By mentally sending out my ki (remember, all the other elements have to be present for ki to be present), I am able to generate greater power. I have also found that this works with jujitsu takedowns and throws. By "thinking" power in the direction I want my opponent to go, I have greater strength in that direction because my energy—my ki—is being projected there.

If you are a hard stylist, keep in mind you won't always have your great power. Such factors as age, illness, and injury will tax and dissipate it. It's in your best interest, therefore, to learn as much as you can about soft-style techniques. The knowledge will add to your external power and help you maintain it when your physical strength wanes.

HOW SOME STYLES DEVELOP POWER

There are about a zillion different martial art systems and styles in the world, give or take a few hundred. The phenomenon of people studying a system for a while and then branching off and creating their own styles is not new; it's been happening for years. This isn't always a bad thing, just when it's done by a martial artist with only a few years of study under his belt.

I had a student who studied with me for seven months and then quit the martial arts—or so I thought. One day, I ran into him in a grocery store and was more than just a little embarrassed for him when I saw that he was wearing a jacket covered with martial art patches, symbols, and hand-painted dragons. He told me he had created his own style and began to brag about how mystical and devastating it was. He even had several students and had told them I was one of his original teachers. I didn't know whether to laugh at him or kick him in the groin. I chose a third option and just walked away shaking my head.

Although these idiots add to the volume of fighting styles out there, most of them fall quickly by the wayside. Other students, legitimate black belt instructors who are sanctioned by their mother schools, have gone out on their own and in time changed certain aspects, eliminated some, and added others. Most of the times these are changes that have added positively to the system.

There are other ways in which styles and systems are formed, but let's not get sidetracked from the issue of power. The bottom line is that over the past 30 years, many new ones have emerged, some of which have stood the test of time.

In this section, we will take a brief look at some well-known fighting arts to see how they develop power overall and how they develop it in specific techniques for which they are recognized. Space limitations allow us to examine only so many fighting arts, and I apologize if I have offended any practitioners by omitting theirs.

I think you will find that although different fighting arts emphasize different techniques, there is a common thread in how they all achieve their power. That fact should not be ignored as you lay out your personal training plan.

Muay Thai

I was attending a Joe Lewis seminar once, and someone asked him what fighting style he thought was the best. Of course, that is an impossible question to answer because styles and systems are made up of individuals: some who train hard, some who don't; some who are gifted, some who are not. But Lewis did say that he thought muay Thai fighters were some of the toughest in the world.

If muay Thai kickboxing isn't the toughest fighting style, it's certainly one of the most painful. Thai kickboxers love to slam their elbows into your cheekbone and kick your head with shins toughened from countless repetitions against kicking shields, wooden posts, and trees.

Let's take a look at how muay Thai fighters develop their roundhouse kick, a technique found in virtually all fighting styles but delivered in a unique fashion by Thai kickers. For instance, they favor the rear-leg roundhouse kick over the front-leg roundhouse. The front-leg kick has been made popular in American karate tournaments over the years since it is faster and closer to the target, and requires less body mechanics to launch. Although it gets

Muay Thai roundhouse power comes from the synchronization of foot pivot, hip roll, leg whip, and arm drop.

points in tournaments, point competitors are not trying to destroy their opponents. Muay Thai fighters are, so they use their rear legs to get more power, then add a unique twist to the kick to make it even stronger. To examine the muay Thai roundhouse kick, let's break it down into four parts: the role of the hips, the support leg, the arms, and the kicking leg.

Thai fighters use a high stance that allows them to move around quickly and kick easily. They frequently switch from right leg forward to left leg to help camouflage the kick's fast launch. They also keep the heel of the rear foot off the floor to help them kick faster. While most martial art styles advocate rotating the hips toward the opponent to add power to the kick, muay Thai fighters go a step further and rotate their hips past the opponent so they can "whip" their leg, often spinning 360 degrees with it.

Rotation of the stationary foot is done much the same as in other styles. Since the Thai fighter is in a relatively high stance and the heel of his stationary foot is already raised, there is little resistance to slow the rotation. The foot rotates as much as 180 degrees, so that its heel points toward the opponent as the kicking leg lands.

Muay Thai kickers use the arms more than other styles to generate greater power in the rear-leg roundhouse kick. Most karate students are taught to keep their hands high throughout the kick so that they are in a position to block an attack and follow up with a counter. Thai fighters, however, believe that whipping an arm downward in the opposite direction opposes the kick's torque and increases its power.

The arm motion is done as follows. Stand in a fighting stance, arms up, with your right leg forward. As you launch your left roundhouse kick, simultaneously whip your left arm down and to the rear. Keep your right fist near your face for protection.

Thai fighters like to strike with the lower portion of the shin as opposed to the top of the foot or the ball of the foot. Striking with a bony leg is painful to the recipient, even when the blow is thrown mildly, and devastating when thrown with power.

Think of the four parts of the Thai roundhouse kick this way. Begin in a high stance and pivot the stationary foot as much as 180 degrees in the opposite direction. As the foot rotates into the turn, begin to turn the hips and then follow with the thigh. An instant later, whip the lower leg around and into the target.

Muay Thai is an ancient fighting art. The majority of its practitioners are slight, so over the years they have learned how to get as much power out of their techniques as possible. The roundhouse kick is one they have truly mastered.

Hapkido

A basic philosophy in the Korean fighting art of hapkido is that even if the opponent blocks the kick, it doesn't matter because its circular power is going to be so great it will cause damage to whatever it hits.

Hapkido was introduced to Korea in the beginning of this century by a Korean martial artist named Yong Shul Choi, who had been studying aiki jujitsu in Japan. It quickly became integrated into Korea's martial arts culture, eventually evolving into a fighting discipline that incorporated the grappling arts of aikido and jujitsu, along with the Korean kicking arts. Hapkido fighters believe that powerful kicks come from natural movement and natural flow patterns, as opposed to the odd and relatively unnatural kicks seen in other styles. Hapkido's premise is that whether you are grappling or striking, power is generated from the circle.

Hapkido fighters believe that although modern-day point karate has created some interesting kicks that can sneak into small places and tag an opponent, such kicks are weak and ineffective on the street. Hapkido kicks, however, travel on a natural path from takeoff to impact, a direct route that maximizes power. For example, power begins to build the moment the foot lifts from the floor and then body momentum is added as it climbs in elevation and arcs toward the target. Then, just inches before impact, the knee snaps the foot the rest of the way to increase the power even more.

Additional power is generated from combination kicking, again following a natural flow of energy. For example, a lead left-leg outside crescent would be followed by a rear right-leg inside crescent. If the opponent is still standing, he would tag on a powerful left spinning crescent or hook kick. Hapkido fighters constantly train to choreograph their kicks to flow automatically from each other in order to generate a tremendous spinning force.

They do little or no faking with their kicks, believing that it exposes them to counterattacks. Their kicks are launched only when there is an absolute belief they will hit the target. They also like to remain in place and let the attacker come to them. They imagine a circle around them that extends out about three feet, and when an opponent enters the circle, they attack.

Shorin-Ryu

Shorin-ryu is a hard Okinawan karate style that proudly calls itself a "one-punch kill style." There are many stories of its masters standing poised for long periods as they waited for the right instant to explode across the gap and smash a pile-driving punch into their opponent. Their punches are so powerful they are often able to penetrate through their opponent's blocks and still land with tremendous force. They rely on great speed to create great power. It's said that the punch of an advanced fighter can travel 43 feet a second and generate 1,500 pounds of force.

Many shorin-ryu fighters supplement their karate training with weight training. Their objective, however, is not to use heavy weights to develop muscular bulk, because they feel that its only value is for moving heavy weights slowly. Most fighters prefer light weights and high repetitions to develop strength that will move a light weight at top speed.

The shorin-ryu stance is a little higher than some Okinawan and Japanese stances, giving the fighter greater mobility to advance and retreat quickly. Its practitioners believe that a strong stance comes from proper body alignment—that is, the hips positioned directly over the legs and the spine held straight.

Shorin-ryu stylists are strong advocates of using hip rotation to drive their powerful reverse punch. But the hips will only turn fast and powerfully if the foundation, the stance, is strong and stable. They also emphasize long-range punches and kicks, since the longer distance allows for a greater development of speed and power in the technique.

Choi li fut's knuckle punch provides more reach and concentrated penetration power.

Kata practice is an important training tool in shorin-ryu because it's a place where stylists train for maximum power in the blocks, kicks, and punches without concern about getting hurt or worrying about what their opponent is going to do back.

Choi Li Fut

Choi li fut is known for its speed and power while using a combination of both hard and soft-style techniques. It's considered hard because it uses powerful punches and kicks, and soft because the power comes from a relaxed body, as opposed to one with hard, contracted muscles. It's also a combination of northern and southern styles, employing relaxed circular hand movements and powerful straight and circular kicks.

Choi li fut gets much of its power from the horse stance and hip rotation. Because it's a weapon-oriented system, students find that the weight of the weapons helps develop good arm and shoulder strength for empty-hand techniques. Although they use a variety of hand techniques, most of them stem from four basic ones.

- *Tsop* is a strike with the middle knuckles of the fingers, giving the fighter a little more reach and more penetration power.
- *Qua* is a backfist motion that uses the entire body to snap the strike forward, particularly the rotation of the hips and shoulders.
- *Jong* is an uppercut technique, using full extension of the arm and a powerful snap of the hips.
- *Sow* is a type of roundhouse punch that draws its tremendous power from the rotation of the waist and hips. It's so powerful that it's considered the knockout technique of the system.

Isshin-Ryu

Literally translated, isshin-ryu, a hybrid Okinawan system, means "one heart or mind technique." Its creator, Tatsuo Shimabuku formed the style in 1954 after years of studying shorin-ryu and goju-ryu. Although the formation of isshin-ryu was heavily influenced by these two styles, Shimabuku added his own touch to make the system his own.

Probably the biggest difference in isshin-ryu from other fighting arts is its use of the vertical punch as opposed to the traditional one where the fist rotates completely over. The vertical punch rotates only one-quarter turn to where the palm faces the inside of the body and the thumb side is

Isshin-ryu stylists believe that the vertical (thumbs up) punch should be snapped back after impact, which transfers more energy into the target.

up. As with the reverse punch, the point of impact with the vertical punch is the two large knuckles.

When the isshin-ryu punch is in the extended position, the inside of the elbow faces up, while the elbow in the standard reverse punch points in. Isshin-ryu fighters believe this variation gives them greater speed and power.

Because there is no twist of the wrist as in the reverse punch, the vertical punch is thought to extend and retract faster. It's believed that by not twisting the arm and wrist, the muscles work in an anatomical line, making for a more natural movement.

Although the standard reverse punch can be snapped back after impact, it's generally left on the target for a brief moment. Isshin-ryu stylists believe this allows for some of its energy to be absorbed back into the arm. The vertical punch, however, is immediately snapped back after it hits the target, not only increasing its speed but also making it difficult for the opponent to grab. It's also believed this makes it more powerful since the snap back transfers greater energy into the target.

Isshin-ryu stylists use the analogy of a man striking a tree with a bat. When a bat is swung full force into the tree, it will break or bounce back and jar the man. But when he snaps the bat back on impact, the blow is more powerful, and there is no jarring sensation because there is less energy being transferred back.

Because the reverse punch locks out, the target has a greater opportunity to move and dissipate the force. The isshin-ryu punch, however, snaps back, leaving less opportunity for the recipient to move away.

Isshin-ryu kicks are generally thrown to low targets in a fast, snapping fashion, employing the same theory as with their fast, retracting punches. The idea is to deliver maximum speed and power to such vulnerable targets as the groin and the knees.

Lama Kung Fu

Lama kung-fu is one of three major schools of the white crane kung-fu system. Its origin, as is the case with many martial art systems, is part mystery, part legend. Most followers believe it was founded by Tibetan Lamaist monks some 300 years ago. Legend has it that one day several monks were watching a white crane fight an ape. While the monks were betting on the ape, the crane plucked out his eye. This so moved the monks that they developed a fighting system using movements from the white crane as their foundation to other kung fu techniques they had already been studying. Although there is much more to lama kung fu's history, for our purposes here, let's take a look at how it uses movement-specific exercises to develop power.

Lama kung fu practitioners make it clear that theirs is a

fighting style, not a martial art used for health, sport, or art. They have maintained the original concept of training for combat reality and, as such, follow these four fighting principles:

1. Totally overwhelm the opponent. When the instant is right, explode into the opponent using full-power movements with one objective: to destroy.
2. Use footwork to "not be there" when the opponent attacks and to strike hard when he is off guard.
3. Penetrate the opponent's defenses by attacking full power over and over again.
4. Intercept the opponent's attack by hitting at the moment he attacks or wait until he commits before counterattacking.

"A powerful body means a powerful weapon," asserts the lama kung fu fighter. With this philosophy in the forefront of his mind, he uses some of the following training methods.

Mok yee pai are bell-shaped, hand-held weights used to add resistance to hand techniques. They are tapered at the top, where there is a handle, and grow wider at the bottom, making them bottom heavy. They can be as light as five pounds, but they gradually increase in weight to whatever the fighter can handle. Mok yee pai weights strengthen the grip, forearm, upper arm, shoulder, and waist. After the limbs have become conditioned, the fighter can add appropriate footwork to the weighted-hand techniques to develop overall coordination with the added weight resistance. For example, a fighter will practice advancing across the room as he executes arm techniques with the mok yee pai.

To develop powerful leg sweeps, the lama kung fu fighter practices sweeps against a six-inch-thick post that is buried in the ground, extending upward about three feet. The post is then wrapped with rope two or three times to give the fighter cushioning.

Sweeps are done either standing or in a squatting position. First one leg sweeps forward against the post, striking it with the shin; then the other leg sweeps around the other way, striking it with the calf. The fighter develops a regular routine of sweeping the post until the leg becomes tough enough that one layer of rope can be removed. The sweep exercise continues until all rope has been removed, leaving the bare post. There have been times when lama kung fu experts have swept a heavy table leg and broken it off.

Forearms are toughened by striking trees repeatedly until the arms are conditioned to withstand tremendous impact. It is said that in times past, some fighters could knock the bark from trees with their forearm strikes.

Shotokan

Shotokan karate is almost synonymous with the words *traditional martial arts.* Many think of this Japanese system as a stiff, robotlike fighting style that uses only a few select techniques to deliver powerful hand strikes and kicks in a linear fashion, straight in and straight out. Although some observers may view this as a weakness in the fighting system, shotokan's early founders and today's practitioners see it as a strength.

Shotokan follows the principle of *ikken hisatsu,* "victory with one blow," as opposed to those fighting styles that believe in hitting multiple times. Target selection is important to the shotokan fighter, and so is great power. Like the samurai philosophy of "one slice, one kill," one solid shotokan reverse punch should be all that is needed to finish a fight.

Like most fighting systems, shotokan uses the entire body to bring out maximum power in a technique. A punch is more than just the fist traveling to a target; it's also the shoulders, the lat muscles, the hips, the abdominal muscles, and the legs.

Many shotokan teachers believe that the reverse punch is the most important technique in all their repertoire. Although it's possible to develop an impressive-looking one in one month, they believe it actually takes years to achieve the one-punch killing power that is the foundation of the art.

Shotokan uses relatively low stances to get as much drive out of the legs as possible. Although this stance appears to offer all the mobility of a huge rock, especially when compared to the loose and mobile fighting postures of some kung fu styles, it's really an illusion: the low stances enable fighters to explode in any direction.

The power of the reverse punch comes from the perfect alignment of the body and the rotation and timing of the hips. Shotokan begins the hip rotation an instant before the punch is launched, believing that it's faster and stronger than turning the hips and punching at the same time.

These fighters develop much of their power through high-repetition training, heavy bag work, hours of hitting the *makiwara* board, and weight training. Because most shotokan stylists maintain a relatively limited repertoire of techniques, they funnel most if not all of their energy into perfecting the basics.

As is the case with many Japanese karate styles, shotokan trains extensively in one-step sparring: the attacker attacks, and the defender blocks and responds with one or more techniques. The shotokan fighter spends hundreds of hours on such training and does so with one thought in mind: victory with one technique.

Pak Mei

Pak mei, also known as "white eyebrow kung fu," relies on power drawn from the practitioner's internal and external energy sources. The power is often referred to as *sacred power* because the body explodes from soft to hard.

Pak mei stylists fight primarily in the middle range, using their hands more than kicks. They maintain relaxed and flexible arms until their blow penetrates into the target. Their power comes from a mastery of external sources—the eyes, mind, hands, waist, and a strong stance—while their internal power comes from the spirit, mental intent, endurance, and ki.

So-called soft power is used to redirect an opponent's attack; then powerful counters are delivered to vulnerable points of the body. Sometimes a counter is done with the same hand that blocks, necessitating that the pak mei fighter switch from soft to hard in an instant.

Pak mei fighters strike with their forearms, open palms, points of their fingers, and their fists, which are held with the middle index knuckle protruding. They believe that the protruding knuckle narrows the penetrating power to a small impact area, being particularly effective against nerve points and other vulnerable body targets.

The spear hand uses either the index and middle finger or all four fingers to deliver a spearlike jab to vital body targets. These fighters condition their body weapons by striking wooden posts and sandbags and by thrusting their hands into buckets of dried beans. With hardened weapons and the proper application of internal and external power, they are able to strike their opponents with total effectiveness.

Eagle Claw Kung Fu

This kung fu style is known for its low stances, beautiful long-fist forms, and unique hand technique called *eagle claw*. The claw is used for grappling in such a way that the attacker experiences extreme pain in the joint, tendons, ligaments, nerves, and even the skin. For example, the eagle claw fighter will grab an attacker's punch by the wrist or elbow and apply a crushing force to it. When the attacker attempts to pull his arm back, he feels even greater pain. Then, while the limb is trapped, the eagle claw fighter punishes the attacker with punches and kicks.

The claw is made by pressing your four fingers together and curling them toward your palm, with your thumb curled and pointing toward the middle finger. The tip of the thumb and the tip of the four fingers should be about two finger-widths apart. The eagle claw can then be used to attack in an upward, sideways, or downward motion. For example, an attacking arm can be painfully grabbed at the wrist with the left hand, while the right hand applies a crushing eagle claw grip at the throat. Eagle claw fighters also use palm strikes, snapping punches, finger strikes, and an assortment of kicks.

Part of the success of eagle claw techniques comes from precise placement of the grab. It's believed that there are more than 300 pressure points on the human body, and of these more than 30 are extremely vulnerable when affected by the great power developed in the eagle claw fighter's hands.

The powerful eagle claw can grab tendons, ligaments, nerves, and skin.

Followers practice several exercises to strengthen the hands. The traditional way was to make the claw formation 100 times every day, starting with the hand open and relaxed, then tensing it hard as the fingers curled into the eagle claw formation. Other traditional exercises include striking with full power against a sandbag with the fingertips. The followers practice high-repetition pushups on their fingertips and thumbs. They practice jar holding in which jars of varying widths and weight are gripped and rotated to exercise the fingers, palms, and wrists (discussed in Chapter 3, "Ancient Exercises"). They also exercise with a long stick to develop flexibility and power in their wrists. The stick is held at one end with the other end pointing straight down to the left. The wrist is rolled so that the end of the stick rotates 360 degrees to the right so that the end points straight down again. Filipino stick fighters call this "motion fanning."

These exercises, combined with modern ones, such as the finger, hand, and forearm exercises listed elsewhere in this book, give eagle claw fighters the tremendous power they use to destroy their opponents.

Wushu

It's not uncommon to get a blank stare in China when you utter the word *kung fu*, but when you say *wushu*, faces brighten and heads nod. Although the word literally means *martial art*, wushu typically is not the aggressive fighting art seen depicted in the old kung fu movies—or the modern ones for that matter.

I had the rare and delightful opportunity to see a wushu demonstration team several years ago as it passed through Portland, Oregon, on the last leg of its U.S. tour. Members of the national team were chosen from throughout China when they were young children and were trained for eight hours every day for several years.

Every member was superlative, far advanced from anything any of us in the audience that night had ever seen in the martial arts. Their punches, kicks, and acrobatic moves were exquisite. The sheer force of their techniques virtually radiated from the stage and into the auditorium. Whether it was the power of their legs as they catapulted themselves through the air, the dexterity and speed in which they maneuvered even the largest and heaviest weapon, or their thunderous footwork as they shot across the stage releasing a barrage of kicks, punches, and weapon strikes, their power was extraordinary.

There are two schools of wushu: the external, whose students practice powerful and vigorous punching, kicking, leaping, and somersaulting techniques; and the internal, which is the practice of soft, flowing techniques that resemble dance movements. Since we are examining the issue of power, let's take a look at a few methods some wushu stylists use to develop their powerful kicking techniques.

Repetition Horse Stance

This exercise develops leg, buttocks, and lower back strength. From the position of attention, slide your left foot out into a deep horse stance as you extend your arms out to the side, your palms up as though you were holding a heavy object. Hold for a moment and breathe in; then turn your palms over as if you were pushing the heavy object down and slowly rise and slide your foot back to position of attention. Repeat for three sets of 10 reps.

Stationary Horse Stance

Sitting in the horse stance is a popular exercise among wushu stylists. Many of them sit for five minutes at a time with their upper thighs parallel with the floor, so low you can set a glass of water on their thighs.

Repetition Forward Stance

From the position of attention, step off to the left with your left foot and assume a deep forward stance. Sink until your upper thigh is parallel with the floor and your hands touch the floor. Take a couple of deep breaths, then push yourself back up to a position of attention. Repeat on the other side. Do two sets of 10 reps.

Stationary Forward Stance

Assume a deep forward stance with the upper leg parallel with the floor, fists clenched at the sides. Just as with the repetition forward stance, your upper body should be maintained straight up and down. Grit your teeth and hold for five minutes. Repeat with the other leg.

Squats

Because students in China don't always have access to weights, they frequently rely on human weight to add resistance to certain exercises, such as the basic squat. It's not uncommon to see wushu students performing squats with one or sometimes two training partners on their shoulders. Do three sets of 10 reps.

Leapfrog Jumps

Wushu stylists believe that leapfrog jumping develops the muscles needed to execute their aerial techniques. Assume a deep squat with your hands on your hips. Using only the power of your legs, spring up as high as you can and as far forward as you can and land in a full squat. Do three sets of 10 reps.

Wushu stylists frequently do squats with human weight.

Kicking

As do the practitioners of most martial art systems, wushu stylists believe in high-repetition kicking exercises. Because they are concerned that too many weight-resistance exercises will build excessive mass and inhibit their kicks, they emphasize hard and fast repetitious kicking to develop speed and power.

They also practice torturously slow kicking. They kick out as slowly as possible and hold the lock-out position for as long as they can tolerate the pain. This strengthens the hips as well as the very leg muscles needed for each kick.

• • •

There are many other systems and styles with fascinating methods of developing power. I encourage you to research them and consider what they have to offer.

CHAPTER THREE

ANCIENT EXERCISES

To those of you who have only trained in martial art schools that are brightly lit, fully equipped with the latest exercise machines, and staffed by personal trainers knowledgeable in the current training and nutrition tricks, here is a bit of information: training hasn't always been that way.

The early masters didn't have treadmills, shiny abdominal machines, pink dumbbells, and squeezie devices to tighten their inner thighs. Instead, they relied on rocks, rope, bags of stones, and whatever else their imaginations could conjure up. With these crude implements, they were able to supplement their training and develop the skills that today are legendary.

Were these devices as beneficial and efficient as modern exercise equipment? My guess is that they were not, but there is no way of knowing for sure because these people have long passed on to that dojo in the sky.

One might argue that old training methods were superior, not because the technology was superior, but because the old masters brought a unique mind-set to their training as a result of their culture, customs, and religion. Many of the old exercises required accepting the premise that they would develop not only exterior power, but internal strength as well. There was an acceptance that internal power and maximum physical power would not come before at least 10 years of continual training.

Let's take a brief look at some of the old training methods and devices. Don't think any less of them because they are old. You may just find something you like or that you can modify to use in your training today.

ELBOW TOUGHENING

Hitting someone with your elbow is like hitting someone with a stick: it hurts no matter where you hit. Here is

Elbow crawling will toughen your elbows, skin, and pertinent muscles.

an old exercise that will effectively toughen the exterior of the joint and strengthen the surrounding muscles.

Lower yourself to the floor so that you are supporting yourself on your elbows and knees. Now crawl. At first, you may need to assist with your legs, but your goal is to walk on your elbows and drag your legs behind you. How much this hurts is directly related to the type of surface you are on. Gravel hurts, but grass is nice.

If you find that you are lowering your forearms and helping with your hands—don't. You want all of the stress to go onto your elbows. One way to prevent using your hands is to hold on to an arnis stick with both hands and hold it up as you crawl.

Evaluate your progress by how far you crawl or how long it takes you. For example, crawl 30 feet, rest, and then do it again for several sets. Or crawl for 30 seconds, rest, and then repeat for however many sets you want to do.

BAG TOSSING

This exercise can still be found in some traditional Chinese styles. The heavy canvas bag is about the size of a pillowcase and filled with ball bearings, 5 to 10 pounds for beginners and up to 30 pounds for advanced students.

The student swings the bag in a pattern of his choice, passing it from one hand to the other. He can swing it up and over his shoulder, across his chest, behind his back, and between his legs. He can also throw it up in the air and catch it in a variety of ways.

Bag tossing can also be done with two people. Face your partner and toss the bag at his shoulder so that he has to rotate his body away to avoid getting hit, but he can still catch it. This teaches the receiver to flow with the momentum but still be quick enough to grab the bag.

Bag tossing exercises the fingers, wrists, forearms, shoulders, and waist.

BRICK HOLDING

This is a forerunner of modern-day exercising with light dumbbells. The bricks were held in the middle and sometimes by the ends.

Hold one in each hand and practice your punches, backfists, and blocks. Never lock out your elbow joints at the extended position. Brick holding was also used to practice kata. Simply hold the bricks and go through all the moves exactly as you would normally.

Brick holding adds power to all of the muscles in the arms, especially gripping muscles.

CHOPSTICK ROLLING

It was believed by Chinese masters that this exercise would develop inner power in the palm-heel strike so that the energy from the blow would travel below the surface of the target. For example, if the blow was delivered to the chest, the force would be transmitted deep into the victim's body, thus causing internal shock.

Bind a bundle of 12 to 15 chopsticks at each end and hold between both palms. Roll the sticks slowly back and forth with tension being maintained from the wrists to the fingertips. According to old beliefs, this should be done for 15 to 60 minutes every day for—are you ready for this? — *10 years.*

EXERCISES FOR DEVELOPING A POWERFUL GRIP

Practitioners of fighting styles that use extensive clawing, gouging, tearing, and other open-handed techniques are especially interested in developing hand and finger strength. This strength is often referred to as *iron hand* or *iron grip*. Here is how they did it before the advent of barbells and dumbbells.

In an exercise called catching the bag, an eight-by-eight-

-inch bag is filled with five pounds of metal shavings or shot and tossed from hand to hand. The bag is tossed straight up in front of the body with one hand and then caught with the other. Move only the lower arms and hands to snatch the bag out of the air and keep the shoulders and upper arms uninvolved and relaxed. Technique is all important to get the maximum benefit. Repeat for five to ten minutes.

When you can do this easily, it's time to increase the weight, but only two to five pounds at a time. Continue in this progression until you can do it with a bag weighing 40 pounds. When that feels comfortable, work on catching it with fewer and fewer fingers until you can do it with just your thumb and one other finger.

The old masters expected their progress in this exercise to take several years. After they had attained it, they advanced to the next phase: the iron ball.

Iron Ball

The concept behind iron-ball exercises is somewhat similar to using wrist weights, but with some additional benefits. With wrist weights, the additional burden is carried primarily by the upper arms and shoulders because the weight is hanging from your wrists, so to speak. Use of the iron ball, however, primarily stimulates the muscles of the wrists, hands, fingers, forearms, and, to a lesser degree, the upper arms and shoulders.

Go to a sporting goods store and pick up a shotput, the iron ball that is used for track and field events. Choose a weight that you can use for three or four sets and eight to ten repetitions. Keep in mind that you are not powerlifting here, but rather adding resistance to familiar movements. Consider an eight- or ten-pound ball to be about average for a fit, adult male. If you require a lighter weight, that's OK. If you think you can go heavier, feel free. Just keep in mind that if your form suffers and you can't do all the sets and reps, the weight is too heavy.

Once you have developed a smooth coordination of handing the iron ball from hand to hand as you did with the bags, it's time to advance to additional exercises with the ball. The goal is the same as with all weight-resistance movements in the martial arts: to add weight progressively to the exercise to build more and more strength. When your body is forced to carry extra poundage through the

Iron-ball punching adds resistance to your hand techniques.

movements, muscle fibers are more deeply stimulated, including some of the surrounding muscles.

One nice side benefit is that the added pounds will make you more aware of how your entire body is used when executing a punch or a block. When the exercises are performed as described, you will develop and become more aware of continuity and flow as you perform repetition after repetition. The added weight will force you to develop a greater awareness of your center, which will enhance your balance and stability as you move. The end result is that you will develop a greater sense of concreteness in your postures from which you will be able to deliver more powerful blows.

When practicing the following movements, and any that you design, perform the complete motion even if that is not the way you normally do it. For example, say you routinely launch your punch from your chest. When you practice with the iron ball, however, begin from a fully chambered position so that you will strengthen the muscles throughout the full range of the movement.

Iron-Ball Punching

Assume a left-leg-forward stance and hold the ball in your right hand in a cocked reverse-punch position next to your hip. Slowly extend your arm out as if punching. At first you may not be able to rotate your hand over as you normally do, and that's OK. Your muscles are still being worked, and eventually you will be able to do so quite easily. Retract the ball about halfway and hand it off to your left hand. Retract your left hand to your hip and then extend it to the locked position. Strive for a smooth flow and a smooth handoff. Don't stop during a set and, as always, rotate your hips.

Do about six punches with each hand before you switch stances and repeat the cycle again. Do a total of four sets.

Iron-Ball High Block

Assume a left-leg-forward fighting stance. Hold the iron ball in your left hand about belt high next to your middle. Slowly raise the ball past your face and extend your arm outward in a standard rising block position. Hold for a second and then lower the ball back to the initial position and switch to your other hand. Then, without hesitation, raise the ball to a high block on the other side.

Do three or four sets of eight to 10 reps of smooth non-stop movement.

Iron-Ball Backfists

You can use whatever stance you want for these, but let's use the horse. Drop into a deep horse stance and face left. Hold the ball in your left hand at about solar plexus level. Extend it outward as if doing a backfist and hold the locked position for a second. Retract the ball to the solar plexus and pass it off to your other hand. Turn to the right and extend the ball out to the locked backfist position.

Continue nonstop, striving for a smooth rhythm. Do three or four sets of eight to 10 reps.

Swinging the Iron Ball

This is a hand- and finger-strengthening exercise rather than a movement directly applicable to a fighting technique. Hold the ball in your right hand as high as you can out to the right and then swing it in an arc down and then up and out to high left. Reach up and grasp the ball with your left hand at high right and then swing it down and up to high left, where you will again change hands.

As your strength progresses, grasp the ball with only four fingers, then three, and finally with just your thumb and index finger. Your goal is to progress to a level where you can do the exercise with a slick substance on the ball, such as cooking oil or hair gel. This forces your muscles to work to hold on to it. *Free tip: wear steel-toed boots.*

The old masters had a good idea with iron-ball training, and it's still applicable today. Pick up two or three different weighted balls and give it a try.

CHINESE TRAINING BALLS

When you buy these golf-ball-sized balls through martial art catalogs or import stores, the instructions usually claim that rolling them in your palm will stimulate certain acupuncture points. This supposedly calms and quiets the spirit and improves your overall health. Sounds a little mystical to me, but I do agree that manipulating them on a regular basis will increase your finger dexterity. And if you do it fast and furious for a given time for three or four sets, your overall hand strength will improve.

Learn to roll the Chinese balls in both directions. Move them as fast as you can for sets of 60 seconds.

Hold two balls in the palm of your right hand and roll them around each other. First go clockwise and then counterclockwise. You will probably be able to roll them more smoothly in one direction than in the other, but with practice you will improve. Once you have developed dexterity, push for more and more speed. Work up to a 60-second set with each hand and do as many sets as it takes to fatigue your fingers.

CHASI

This is a long-handled rod with a weight attached to one end. In the old days, a stone with a hole was used so the handle could be attached to it. Today, you can use a can filled with cement, or you can simply place barbell plates on one end of a long or short bar.

The *chasi*, a unique device that attacks the forearm muscles at angles other exercise can't reach, is primarily used to develop the forearms and the wrists.

Stand at attention and hold the chasi straight down at your side, the thumb side of your fist to the front. Roll your fist upward as you simultaneously bend your elbow and raise your forearm just a little past horizontal. Do three sets of 10 reps with each arm.

A second exercise is to bend your elbow and bring your forearm up until it's parallel with the floor. Slowly, so as not to strain your wrist, rotate the chasi to the left and then roll it back over to the right. Hold your elbow as still as you can so that it's not doing the work. This is a particularly good exercise for arnis fighters. Do three sets of 10 reps.

HORSE STANCE

The horse stance is probably one of the oldest stances and exercises in the martial arts; its likeness can be seen in ancient paintings and sculptures of Chinese, Japanese, and Korean warriors. It has survived the test of time because it's a good fighting stance and it develops power in the legs.

The modern method of using the horse stance as an exercise is discussed later in this book. For now, let's take a brief look at some of the ways it was used in days of old. I would use caution when experimenting with these old horse exercises because they are not all physically sound and some of them may cause injury.

Long Sitting

The value of sitting in the horse stance for long periods is questionable as a physical exercise, but without a doubt it will test your mental fortitude. There are many stories in martial art folklore of students and masters sitting in a horse stance for two hours, four hours, all day, and even barefoot in the snow. Usually they had to be carried away afterward.

Will this make the legs stronger? Possibly, if done regularly and systematically. But who has the time? For sure, it will cause great pain, but it may cause temporary or long-term injury as well. Contrary to what some of the old masters taught, sitting in horse stance for long stretches is unnecessary, but, as we shall see later, sitting for short durations will develop power.

First, let's see how they used to do it.

Partner-Assisted Horse Stance

This is an old way to add resistance to the horse stance to build strength in the legs—supposedly.

It was common for students to choose partners and take turns sitting on each other's shoulders. The bottom person would then sit in a horse stance and hold a fixed position. Sometimes the rider would stand on the sitter's thighs and hold on to his shoulders.

The partner-assisted horse stance might be of benefit if you practice it on a regular basis, with a progressive increase in weight, and while sitting in high, medium, and low positions. The varying positions are important because the horse stance only strengthens the legs in the position in which it's held. If you only sit in a low position, it will not strengthen your legs for a higher position. More on this later.

The partner-assisted horse stance is potentially dangerous. It's important that the rider sit motionless and not engage in horseplay, so to speak. A sudden shift in weight can cause injury to the bottom student.

Sitting While Holding Weights

A common exercise in days of old was to sit in a horse stance while holding a pole across the shoulders. Buckets of water or bags of stones hung from the ends of the pole, which added resistance to the horse stance. Two other variations were to hold weighted buckets in the hands and place bags of rice on the shoulders.

These are all acceptable forms of resistance (today you can use dumbbells and barbells) and are beneficial only as long as you practice the exercise two or three days a week at a variety of heights.

Moving Horse Stance

This old exercise is still used today in some of the more traditional schools (my daughter created an excellent variation that is illustrated in Chapter 11). The moving horse stance is a good power developer, but only if practiced regularly.

Assume a horse stance facing north. Move your right foot over to your left, turn to your left 90 degrees, slide your right foot to the right, and settle into a horse stance facing west. Hold for a second and then do the same footwork again, this time settling into a locked position facing south, the opposite direction from where you started. Do it again, ending in an easterly direction, and one last time to face north again. To move the other way, step off with your left foot as you execute each turn to the right.

You can also move forward and backward in the horse stance. Assume the stance facing north. Move your right foot up to your left and continue until you are locked into a horse stance facing south. To advance again, move your left foot up to your right and contin-

Horse sitting with a partner strengthens your legs only in the position you are sitting.

ue moving it forward until you are once again facing north. To move backward, simply reverse the process.

Once you catch on to moving in the horse stance, and it won't take long, you can move all over the room in any fashion you want, forward and backward. Maintain the same height so that your head doesn't bob up and down as you change positions. Move 10 times into high horse, 10 into medium, and 10 into deep horse.

When you perform three of four cycles in the three levels, you will have taxed your legs about as much as you will want to.

Modern versions of using the horse stance as an exercise will be discussed later.

HANGING EXERCISE

This is an old ninjitsu exercise used to develop hand and arm strength so that ninjas could hang for long periods whenever the spy business called for it. Although there are few situations today that require you to hang for long periods, the exercise will quickly develop hand strength and endurance. It doesn't matter whether you hang from a bar, tree branch, or beam, other than that the different thicknesses will activate different muscles.

The concept is simple: you hang as long as possible. For example, try one set for 60 seconds. Let's say you were successful and after a few seconds of rest you do another set, but this time you only last 40 seconds. To progress, work to increase the second set to 60 seconds over the next few workouts. Then add a third set, hanging for as long as you can. Continue to work on the third one until you can hang for 60 seconds. After reaching this goal, you can add a fourth set or increase the number of seconds in each of the first three sets.

This is not an easy exercise; in fact, it's quite unpleasant. But it will strengthen and add power to your grip, forearms, and, most assuredly, your discipline.

JAR HOLDING

To do this ancient exercise, fill a jar or vase with water or sand, the amount depends on the strength of your grip. Then grasp the top of the jar and rotate it as far as you can to the left then as far as you can to the right. As your strength increases, so should the contents. This is a good isometric exercise for the fingers and a good isotonic exercise for the wrists. Do three sets of 10 rotations.

IRON GETA

The *geta* is a type of sandal that was worn in old Japan and is still occasionally worn today by some traditional Japanese. Though most were made of wood, geta made of iron were worn by some martial artists as a way to add resistance to their kicks. They

Hanging for 60-second sets will develop hand and arm strength

Fill the jar with water or sand and rotate it as far as you can in both directions.

were used regularly by martial artists in Japan 30 years ago and are still used by staunch traditionalists in Asia and even here in the United States. They are the forerunner of modern-day ankle weights, though more cumbersome and dangerous because they can fly off the foot and injure innocent passersby.

If the fighter can keep them on his feet, he can use them for resistance in all kicking movements. They can also be held in the hands to add resistance to punching and striking exercises.

If you can find a pair, and that's not easy to do, train using the same sets and reps as when practicing with ankle weights.

• • •

There are many other ancient exercises that can be found in literature and in a scattering of schools. Some of the exercises are just plain dangerous, while others may have some value. If you find something that looks interesting and there is any question in your mind that it might be physiologically unsound, don't use it. Get advice from your instructor first or from anyone else who is knowledgeable in exercise science.

CHAPTER FOUR

WEIGHT-RESISTANCE EXERCISES

Supplementing martial arts training with weight training was more controversial several years ago than it is today. Yet, despite the reams of information about the benefits of weight-resistance exercises for athletes, some people still believe that such training will make them muscle-bound or otherwise negatively affect their martial arts.

Some people even believe that fighting knowledge alone will make up for their lack of physical strength and make them equal to a powerful assailant. Martial artists who believe these things are dealing with antiquated and unrealistic information and limiting their capabilities in their martial art.

Besides the disbelievers and the ill informed, there are other people, making up perhaps the largest group, who have not trained with weight-resistance exercises. These are students who have either never given any thought to supplementing their training with weights or, if they have, who lack the knowledge to put together an applicable weight-training program.

To this last group of people and to those who still follow old belief systems, I am going to try my darnedest to get you to accept this fact: *Modern, scientific weight training concepts and principles will dramatically improve your fighting ability and increase your chance of winning in sport and in the street.*

Though I firmly believe this and have witnessed countless examples over my 30-plus years in the martial arts, it's also a belief system adhered to by thousands of other martial artists, most modern-day masters, and some masters of old. *Proper weight training will have a remarkably positive effect on your techniques by making them stronger, faster, and able to last longer in a fight.*

Will big muscles slow you down? Yes, if your muscles are bloated way beyond the norm, such as those people pictured in the bodybuilding magazines. Physique competitors train for excessively large muscles, and many of them take steroids to get them even larger. Such development is not the purpose of this book. If it is your goal to develop huge size, then you should pursue the volumes of information available on the market to do just that. You will not find such information here, since 19-inch arms and 30-inch thighs serve no valuable function in the martial arts and most likely would be detrimental to speed and muscle fluidity.

WHY EXERCISE WITH WEIGHTS?

For our purposes here, the objective of supplementing martial arts training with weight lifting is to increase the power of your punches, kicks, blocks, and grappling.

Muscle Fibers

One nerve impulse can stimulate hundreds of muscle

fibers at one time. Through weight training, you will increase the number of motor nerves and muscle fibers that can be stimulated at any given moment. You will also increase and balance strength in all the muscles you are using, so that your nervous system can draw upon a greater variety of fibers. That way when one group of fibers tire, another group kicks in and relieves them.

Nerves and Strength

At the risk of seeming a little silly, think of your nerves as tiny messengers on bicycles riding to your muscle fibers and telling them to twitch and do something. If the messengers don't get to the fibers, you will stand motionless while your opponent thumps you at will. But because you train in the martial arts, the messengers get through, bringing information to your muscle fibers as to how many to use, whether to use fast twitch or slow twitch, in what order to use them, and for how long. Your little messengers will do exactly what you have taught them to do.

Let's say you have been practicing your kata at top speed several times a week in an effort to increase your speed and strength. You have improved so much that you decide to compete in a tournament the following Saturday. At the competition, you tell yourself that you need to impress the judges with your speed and power. This sets into motion your little bicycling messengers to do as they have been trained to do: deliver messages to your fast-twitch muscles to move at top speed.

You impress the judges enough to tie for first place, and you have to do your 100-move kata again. Once more your messengers pedal madly to your fast-twitch muscles. Again you tie, and the judges ask you to do it again. This time, when the messengers arrive at the fast-twitch muscles, they find the muscles pooped out. The messengers should be going for help from the slow-twitch, endurance muscles, but the messengers have not been taught to do that. They have only been instructed to go to the muscle fibers that make the techniques move fast. As a result, when you go through the kata again, your energy has dissipated and your speed and strength are no longer there because you have never trained your muscles for hard endurance work.

What all this means is that it's important to train for speed, power, *and* endurance so that your nervous system, those little messengers, can call on a variety of muscle fibers to give your martial art techniques the right kind of strength for the situation you are in.

Some Side Benefits

In the following pages, we will examine a number of weight-training concepts and principles that will increase your strength in the martial arts dramatically. Your objective is not to gain strength for strength's sake, but to develop power in your punches, kicks, blocks, and grappling.

Stronger Connectives

Weight training will strengthen the tendons and ligaments that surround your joints—especially beneficial because karate is so hard on them. When you launch a hard, full extension punch into the air, it's your ligaments and tendons that stop your arm and save your elbow joint from hyperextending. Have you ever had the not-so-wonderful experience of throwing a hard punch or kick at a bag and missing? Your tendons and ligaments didn't stop the blow because your intention was to punch into the bag. I've done it so hard a couple of times that I haven't been able to use my arm and leg for several days afterward. It's a special way to feel really stupid.

A ligament's job is to connect bones to other bones, and a tendon's job is to attach bones to muscles. Weight training won't help you if you miss the bag, but it will keep your ligaments and tendons healthy and strong and able to stop your kicks and punches before the joints takes the full, jarring impact.

Weight training and stretching increase your joint mobility.

Increase Joint Mobility

Martial art movements ask a lot of your joints. When you reach way out to tag your opponent with a backfist, or when you launch your side kick at your opponent's nose, you are placing tremendous stress on your joints—especially if you haven't been training specifically for those extended movements.

Weight training, in conjunction with your stretching exercises, will increase your mobility and greatly reduce your chance of going beyond your given range of movement. In addition, weight-resistance exercise will strengthen the joint and allow the limb to move farther and faster.

Increase Bone Density

If you didn't have enough bone density, the bones in your forearm would crumble the first time you blocked your opponent's kick; the bones in your legs would shatter when you kicked the heavy bag or when you landed after a jump kick; and the bones in your neck would crack like fine china when your opponent tagged your forehead with a backfist.

More than any other type of exercise, weight training, in conjunction with a healthy diet, will increase your bone density.

This is all internal physiological stuff, but it's nonetheless extremely important to your complete martial art development. If you were building a house and you didn't build a strong foundation, all the pretty paint, cute shutters, and thermal glass panes wouldn't matter because the house would quickly break down and be out of commission. The same is true of you: if you don't strengthen your body internally, great power will never be yours.

VARYING YOUR WEIGHT-TRAINING EXERCISES

Perhaps the biggest reason to change your exercises frequently is to prevent getting physically and mentally stale. Some professional lifters vary their routine in some fashion every third workout, while others find that changing once a month is enough to keep them physically and mentally charged.

When you do the same exercise for a long time, you risk overdeveloping as well as underdeveloping the target muscle. For example, if you only do bench presses, you will overdevelop the belly of the pec muscle but leave the upper, under, and outside portion underdeveloped. But by using a variety of exercises, you develop a more complete and, therefore, stronger muscle.

By varying your exercises and frequently changing your workout, you reduce the chance of getting hurt. Let's say you are in a clinch with your opponent and pushing against him, a move that uses the strength of the inner-pec muscles of your chest. Your opponent suddenly sidesteps a little, enough to shift the stress from your inner pec to your outer pec, which has not been strengthened to the same degree. The result is that you are unable to push with the weaker muscle as hard as you did with the more developed muscle. Even worse, you may experience a sharp pain in your outer chest, the result of a strain, pull, or tear when all the stress shifts to a weaker muscle.

A War Story

While on patrol one day, I spotted a guy on a street corner stabbing another guy in the temple with an ice pick. I called for backup, scrambled out of my police car, jumped over a four-foot-high chain fence, and grappled the stabber down to the sidewalk. Then the delirious, bloody, and enraged victim tried to get at the stabber, and I scuffled with him, taking him to the cement. The stabber tried to get up, and I dumped him again, wanting to keep him down since I had not yet taken the ice pick away from him. As I struggled with the attacker, his victim was crawling toward us, screaming at me to get out of his way so he could get the guy. As I was blocking his path and trying to bring some control to the situation, my backup pulled up.

By now, the stabber had crawled under the fence to the curb and was trying to get to his feet. The backup officer, who didn't know what was going on and hadn't seen the ice pick in the man's hand, began to help him up. Concerned for the officer's safety, I pushed the victim away, reached over the fence, and grabbed a tight handful of the stabber's hair, while warning the officer of the man's weapon.

(Let me interrupt this tale to say that for several months before that day, I had been training hard for a tournament. Part of my routine was to do flat bench presses, a wonderful exercise, but one that mostly works the center of the pec muscle. Back to the story.)

I like hair techniques because they cause acute but temporary pain and provide excellent control and direction to a resisting suspect. The reach across the fence was awkward because of my off-balance body position. Nonetheless, I gave the guy's hair a twist and dumped him on his back like a dropped bag of potatoes. Because of my awkward stance, however, my outer-pec muscle, the portion I had not been training, went *twang*, like a broken guitar string.

The bad guy went to jail, the victim nearly died, and I spent weeks in an arm sling. I missed the tournament, too.

KINDS OF RESISTANCE TRAINING

For our purposes here, we will be looking at various isometric and isotonic exercise routines and concepts about how they develop power in martial art techniques. An isometric exercise is a motionless muscular contraction, such as when you press outward against a door facing. An isotonic movement is what we generally think of when lifting weights—that is, moving a weight from point A to point B, such as when you curl a barbell from your thighs to your shoulders.

Isometric

Pitting your strength against an immovable object strengthens your muscles only in the position you are working at the moment.

Read that last sentence again to make sure that important point is absolutely clear. Whatever position you are in when doing an exertion in an isometric exercise, that is the only point you are exercising. If you are pulling at a bar at the midway point in a curl, you are not exercising the muscles involved at the beginning position, a quarter-way through it, three-quarters, or at the completion of the curl. In order to work the entire range of the muscle, you must do an isometric exercise in at least three stages. Some authorities advocate breaking the stages into six parts, sometimes even eight.

There are two advantages to isometric exercises: (1) they require little in the way of special equipment, which makes them affordable and easy to do just about anywhere; (2) they are an effective way to increase strength in one phase of a martial art movement, say, the beginning of the backfist or in the front kick's lockout position.

Of course, there are also disadvantages. Strenuous pushing and pulling against a fixed object can elevate your blood pressure dramatically. If you are just starting an exercise routine, you should check with your doctor to see whether there are any particulars about your health that need to be addressed. Be sure to tell the doctor that you will be incorporating isometrics. Another disadvantage is that muscles worked isometrically don't tire at the same rate as when doing other types of exercise. This increases the possibility of overexerting a muscle to the point of injury.

But back to the positive. Isometric exercises can be beneficial when injury prevents other types of training. Several years ago, I injured the nerves in my lower left biceps while arresting a protester at a demonstration. To this day, standard curling motions still cause great pain and numbing in my arm. The only exercises I have been able to do are isometric curling positions and some dynamic tension movements (dynamic tension is discussed in Chapter 7).

I do two sets each of narrow, medium, and close grips on the bar, in five positions: (1) in front of the thighs, (2) one-quarter up, (3) halfway, (4) three-quarters, and (5) all the way up. I proceed through all five stages using the close grip, then with a medium grip, and again using a wide grip. I always stretch a little or just rest for 20 seconds between each stage. Practicing isometrics has given me greater tone and strength than I would have otherwise had. (More on isometrics in a moment.)

Isotonic

This is the most well-known type of weight-resistance exercise. For example, lying on your back and pressing a barbell up from your chest and then returning it to your chest is an isotonic exercise called the bench press. Usually, an isotonic exercise involves the muscle's complete range of movement, as opposed to an isometric exercise which works only one stage of it.

Equipment for isotonic exercise is easy to find. You can join a health club, buy your own weights, or find a community facility where you can use equipment for free.

But there are some disadvantages to isotonic exercises that you should keep in mind. With some exercises, tension on the muscles changes throughout the move. The barbell curl is the most obvious example. When you begin to curl the weight upward in an arc from a straight-down position, maximum stress on your biceps occurs around 120 degrees, a position about halfway between horizontal with the floor and all the way up. Once you move the weight past that point, the tension is reduced as gravity and momentum take over. However, you may use cables, pulleys, and any other types of exercise machine designed to maintain constant tension throughout the movement to get around this problem.

Cable curls provide constant tension throughout the full range of an exercise.

One other significant disadvantage is that isotonic weight exercises can be hard on your body if you are not careful. Lowering the weight is particularly stressful on muscles, tendons, and joints. In fact, whenever you get sore from a new exercise, it's usually from the lowering phase, not the lifting phase. However, the lifting phase can be injurious if it's done awkwardly. And as with isometric exercises, your blood pressure will elevate.

Although there are many isometric and isotonic weight-resistance routines, we will be looking at those that specifically build power in your fighting techniques. There are many fighters who do not understand that to develop a powerful front kick and a powerful reverse punch, they must use resistance exercises for those exact motions. For example, bench presses will develop strength in your chest, triceps, and shoulders, but will only indirectly benefit your backfist strikes since the bench press motion is not the same as the backfist motion. Likewise, squats will help your front kick, but will only indirectly benefit your sidekick.

The goal throughout this text is to provide you with training techniques that are directly applicable to specific punches, kicks, and blocks.

BASIC LIFTING RULES

If you are a beginner at weight training, follow these rules religiously for at least six months. Doing so will reduce the chance of injury and ensure rapid gains in power.

- Stand straight and avoid rocking your body, thrusting your hips, or in any other way assisting a repetition. Not only does this defeat your purpose, but it may cause injury.
- Each repetition should take about four seconds; two in the lifting phase, two for lowering.
- Work the full range of the repetition from full stretch to peak contraction.
- Never hold your breath; breathe normally.
- Each set should consist of eight repetitions. If you can't do eight, decrease the weight until you can. When you have worked up to 12 reps, you have gained strength, and it's time to increase the weight by about 5 percent.
- Unless you are tired, try to increase one repetition every workout or every other workout.

- Rest no more than 30 seconds between sets.
- Work every major muscle group. Not working a muscle group can lead to unbalanced development and injury.
- Do about three sets for each exercise.
- Exercise the large muscles first and work your way to the smaller muscle groups. For example, exercise your chest first, then proceed through your back, legs, shoulders, arms, and neck.

After six months of preconditioning your muscles, slowly incorporate various concepts and any of the advanced exercises discussed later.

As mentioned, the concepts, principles, and routines that follow are all applicable to martial art movements. There are others that I haven't illustrated only because of space limitations. But I feel confident that after examining the routines and ideas in this book, you will learn enough to create your own exercises and recognize others that fit the criteria.

When considering other training regimens, keep in mind that you can't look at a routine or training concept in a book or magazine and say with accuracy that it will work for you. Maybe it will, maybe it won't. People respond differently to exercise for a variety of reasons. The only way you are going to know is to try it and see. Give a new exercise or concept 12 weeks. If you are training correctly and at 100 percent of your effort, but growth is just not happening, then you need to modify or change completely and experiment further.

A word of caution: Don't follow the routine of some steroid freak in a glossy bodybuilding magazine. If, in fact, there is any truth to the Herculean lifting routines in these magazines, these "champions" are able to do them because of their years of training and their regular consumption of harmful drugs. Following their training regimens can lead to overtraining or injury. Use the magazines to learn about exercises that relate to your martial art training but leave the routines alone.

HOW TO HELP YOUR SORE MUSCLES RECOVER

Here are some ways to recover from a new weight-resistance workout or an especially grueling one. Muscle soreness and next-day fatigue are inevitable in weight training, but there are ways to make it a little easier on yourself.

Try working out again. It's true, this seldom-used device will get you going in the morning when you are feeling wiped out from a hard workout the day before. Whether you are trashed from a heavy weight-training session or a hard martial art workout, a little early-morning training the following day will leave you feeling more energized than a double shot from the corner espresso stand.

But feeling good isn't the primary reason to raise a sweat in the morning. Waste products build up in your body after a vigorous workout, and vital nutritional elements are reduced. It's not uncommon after an extremely taxing workout for the body to require several days to recuperate. A light workout will help flush out the waste products from your tired body and get your sluggish blood flowing into your stiff muscles. This will give you a shot of energy to get your day going and speed up the recuperative process to prepare you for your next training session.

If you are a runner, do a short run, about 20 to 30 minutes, or go for a moderately paced walk, again for 20 to 30 minutes. Don't push it. This is only a feel-good workout.

Go through a kata a couple of times. Perform the moves at slow to medium speed and use shallow stances so as not to tax your already tired legs.

Consider stretching to lubricate your muscles with fresh blood. This is not a session to push for greater flexibility, but rather to loosen the muscles, joints, and ligaments. Your objective is to get your blood flowing and give yourself a jump start. By the way, an easy 15-minute

Light stretching lubricates the muscles and flushes out fatigue and soreness.

stretch when you first get home from a hard day at work is a great way to give yourself a shot of energy for your evening activities.

Abdominal exercises are also an excellent early morning exercise. Think of them as working the center of your body to send invigorating blood all the way up to your head and all the way down to your toes. A nice side benefit is that you get to start out the day with a tight midsection.

Whatever activity you choose, do it for about 10 to 15 minutes. This is an easy workout, something that will ease the pain a little without having to take a pill.

WEIGHT-RESISTANCE ROUTINES

Hitting power is only one benefit of weight-resistance training for the martial arts.

A strong, weight-trained fighter is hard to move, hard to drive back. It's as if his strength has rooted him into the earth, stabilizing him and reducing the chance he will get knocked off balance. A covering of muscle mass can act almost like a shield, providing additional protection against an attacker's body blows. Ask yourself this: If you are going to get kicked in the chest, would you rather have a chest like Arnold Schwarzenegger's or a sunken chest and a protruding rib cage? A fighter who has developed visible muscle mass and physical strength has an attitude of greater confidence than a person in poor physical condition. His appearance and his confident attitude are often enough to discourage a would-be attacker. Put yourself in the attacker's shoes for a moment: Would you go after the pencil-necked, spaghetti-armed guy with his ribs showing or the thickly built guy with a demeanor that says, "Let's get it on"?

In this section we are going to examine several weight-training concepts that have been proven to develop power in martial art techniques. Keep in mind that not every concept or routine is going to benefit every person. Chances are good that if 10 people try any given concept or routine, only eight will benefit from it. What works for one fighter may not always work for another. Or a routine might work for you this year, but your body won't respond next year. On the flip side, a routine may not work for you now but will work like a charm in 12 months.

Keep an open mind and stay in tune with your body. Monitor your results, or lack of results, and remember that your body is one of a kind. It ebbs and flows; it responds and it doesn't respond.

Make it your goal to develop the power to punch and kick as hard as a fighter in the weight class above you. If you are a lightweight, train to hit as hard as a middleweight; if you are a middleweight, train to hit as hard as a heavyweight fighter. Imagine your opponent's surprise.

Let's begin this section with a brief look at the routines of Bruce Lee and jujitsu great Royce Gracie.

Bruce Lee

One look at Bruce Lee's phenomenal physique and it's

obvious that he was no stranger to weight training. But Lee didn't lift just to look good. He trained for what he called "real world power," power directly applicable to his martial art training. He believed that the value of power lay in a fighter's ability to use it in his punches and kicks. He saw little value in big muscles if the person could lift tremendous pounds in the gym but was unable to channel it into his fighting techniques. He was 100-percent committed to maximizing his power through weight training and continued doing it until he died on July 20, 1973. Just look at some of his power feats.

- He could lunge across a three-foot span and strike a target in five-hundredths of a second.
- He could do push-ups on one finger, using only one hand.
- He could hold a 125-pound barbell against his chest while standing, then slowly extend the weight straight out and hold it there. He was once timed extending a 70-pound barbell for 20 seconds. This was done at a body weight of 138 pounds.
- He could lift a 70-pound dumbbell laterally to his side and hold it straight out for several seconds.
- He could thrust his fingers through the side of an unopened pop can.
- He could destroy a 100-pound bag with a side kick.
- He could kick a 300-pound bag so hard it would hit the ceiling.
- He could strike a man 100 pounds heavier from a distance of only one inch and knock the man back 15 feet—without first retracting the punch.
- He could place his palm on a man's chest and, with a twitch of his muscles, send the man flying.
- He once punched and caved in protective headgear made from heavy steel rods. Previous attempts to dent the headgear with a sledgehammer had failed.

Bruce Lee didn't get involved with weights until late in his career. But when he saw the results he was getting, he jumped into it with both feet. After some trial and error, Bruce used a thrice-weekly weight training schedule, and sometimes one that was two days on, two days off. This allowed him to practice his martial arts on other days, as well as work on his flexibility and cardiovascular training. All this provided him with a well-rounded workout.

Bruce followed a basic program of three sets per exercise, 15 reps per set. He liked to use cables and experiment with different angles. Sometimes he used a heavy-day, light-day routine, pushing for heavy poundage one training day, then doing high reps with low weights the next.

He found that partial reps enhanced his explosive power. For example, he liked to work just the last three inches of the bench press, using as much weight as he could handle. This is a concept that approximates the last inches of a punch, where the fist is moving at its greatest velocity and is a microsecond away from tensing on impact.

Bruce also experimented with resistance movements that were specific to his martial arts. For example, he favored a 12-set, 1,200-rep punching drill that would probably destroy the arms and shoulders of most fighters. He would begin with one-pound dumbbells, executing 100 punches with each arm, and do another 100 reps with two-pound dumbbells, then with three-, five-, seven-, and ten-pound weights. Then he would go back down the scale, executing 100 reps with ten-, seven-, five-, three-, two-, and one-pound weights, finishing with a final set of 100 punches without weights.

Many martial artists who knew or trained with Bruce Lee still speak of his fantastic forearms. Linda Lee, Bruce's wife, says that he was a "forearm fanatic." He would do some kind of exercise for them every day, believing they were so tough and thick that they could tolerate the extreme training. He favored all kinds of grip-type exercises, barbell wrist curls, and leverage dumbbells that have plates loaded on just one end.

Few people would argue that Bruce Lee was a martial

art superstar, a true master who picked up the martial art world by its ankle and gave it a serious shake. His persona, his skill, and his incredible physique showed us what was possible and what we could strive for. Without a doubt he brought a certain amount of natural ability to his beloved art, but he also trained hard, perhaps harder than most. And weight training was a big part of his regimen.

Royce Gracie

Royce Gracie, who has skyrocketed to fame in recent years as a result of his wins in the televised Ultimate Fighting Championships, incorporates a weight-training program designed to increase power and speed in his jujitsu techniques.

As of this writing, he trains twice a week, believing that it's best to undertrain than overtrain and risk injury. The basis of his program is to develop speed and strength by using 80 percent of his maximum weight per exercise and perform each repetition as fast as possible. This is a system used by some of the world's top athletes.

When Gracie performs a pushing exercise, such as the upward motion of the bench press, he drives the weight up fast, exploding to full extension of his arms. He lowers the weight at normal speed and then explodes upward with it again. It is this explosiveness that stimulates the fast-twitch muscles necessary for speed and power. When he can do five reps easily, he increases the weight.

Gracie uses super sets to save time. For example, he does a set of bench presses and then immediately does a set of barbell curls. Unlike standard bodybuilding where the lifter rests 15 to 30 seconds between exercises, Gracie rests a full five minutes between super sets. This allows his muscles to recuperate and gather strength to explode on the next set of exercises.

OTHER ROUTINES AND CONCEPTS

Use this section to start thinking and planning how you

want to incorporate weight training into your personal program. The following routines and concepts have been included here because they will increase your fighting power. You may use them as is or modify them to fit your personalized routine. The actual weight-resistance exercises are sprinkled throughout the chapters that follow.

Surprise Your Muscles

Know that muscles are living cells and, as such, respond to all stimuli. They respond fast, but they adapt quickly too. Understanding this is an important key to increasing your power. For example, if you always do barbell curls with 80 pounds, your muscles soon adjust, you reach a plateau, and your progress stops. But when you bump the weight up to 90 pounds, your biceps must immediately make an adjustment, and in short order you develop more strength and power. Progressively increasing poundage is one basic way to progress.

But here is the bad news. You won't progress this way forever. Eventually you are going to reach your potential, a point where you can't add more weight. You are going to have to do something different.

One way is to keep surprising ("shocking" in bodybuilding parlance) your muscles. Don't let them get used to a routine, rep count, poundage, weekly schedule, order of exercises, rest time, or the time of day you train. The surprise doesn't have to be big; it just has to be different enough so that your muscles raise their little eyebrows and ask, "What is this?" (assuming of course that your muscles have little eyebrows).

In my training, I like to tackle a new routine at the beginning of each month. If I have found an exercise that is working for me and can't bear to stop doing it yet, I still modify it some way. I use lighter weights and higher reps, heavier weights and fewer reps, or combine it with another exercise or any number of other modifications to keep it fresh and effective.

In this section, I have included a few ways to surprise your muscles and stimulate them into rapid growth. I think you will find these unique and productive.

Slow Reps

I know this isn't a positive thing to say, but you will hate slow reps. Everyone who tries them does, but everyone who does them correctly loves the results they get. There are two simple variations you can do: a hard one and a harder one. Both versions involve counting to yourself, or out loud, as you do each rep of an exercise.

To do the hard version, count slowly "one-thousand-one, one-thousand-two" on the positive half of the rep, such as when you curl the weight up or when you press a weight overhead, and then count "one-thousand-one, one-thousand-two, one-thousand-three, one-thousand-four" on the negative portion when you lower the weight. If you have trouble with your mind wandering when you train, this approach will teach you to focus on the task. At first, you may find that you can't use your normal poundage or do as many repetitions, but after a few workouts you should be back to your normal weight and rep count.

Now for the harder version. You should have at least six months of training experience before you attempt this. The good news is that you do only one set per body part per workout, such as one set of curls for the biceps. The bad news is that the set is a screamer.

Warm up your body as you normally do before you start lifting. Now, using curls again as an example, do your one and only set this way: as you curl the weight up, count "one-thousand-one, one-thousand-two . . . one-thousand-ten." This means it takes you ten seconds to complete the positive portion of the curl. To lower it, your count goes up to one-thousand-five, five full seconds to descend. Do 10 reps this way.

You can use this approach to work your entire body, using only one set per body part. You will have to reduce your normal poundage by about 20 percent, but by the time you get to the last rep it will feel as if you have doubled the poundage. Your entire routine will only take about 30 minutes, but you will feel as if you have been training for hours. Give yourself 48 hours of rest before you lift again. This rest period is imperative because, without it, you will not increase your power.

A variation is to count to one-thousand-five on the positive and one-thousand-ten on the negative. Some lifters do ten and five one month then switch to five and ten the next. I like to give my ol' bod a break and reward it with something completely different for a month, such as speed reps, or dead stops, and then return to slow reps.

Speed Reps

Speed reps shock your muscles into growth, increasing your power and stimulating your fast-twitch muscles.

Here is how it works using the bench press. Let's say you can bench that 100-pound bar 25 times at normal speed within 60 seconds. But if you pumped out the reps fast, you could do a lot more, probably 35 or 40. By using speed, you generate more power in a limited time frame, forcing your muscles to push harder and, in the end, grow stronger.

When performing speed reps, you must continually push to increase the number of reps in the 60-second period. If you can do 30 benches today, push to do 31 in your next workout. Each time you manage one additional rep in the same time frame, you force your muscles to grow and increase their power.

The trick is to find the appropriate weight to use for each exercise in which you use speed reps. If you can't do 20 reps with a weight for 60 seconds at a normal pace, then reduce the weight. If you can do 20 reps easily within the time limit, you need to add weight. When you have found a weight that you can bench at least 20 times in 60 seconds at medium speed, stick with it and begin to progressively increase the number of reps.

Don't immediately push yourself to go as fast as you

can. This will result in extreme soreness and put you at risk of injury. Instead, do 21 or 22 reps on your next workout, then 23 on the one after that, and so on.

Pump out the reps in a nice smooth groove. No matter what exercise you are doing—curls, shoulder presses, bentover rowing—you want to pump out the reps like a well-greased machine. It's even permissible to cheat a little toward the end of the minute, as long as you don't get carried away and cheat so much that your target muscles are no longer getting worked.

One set of the exercise is sufficient. Start with a couple of light-weight sets of benches to warm up your muscles and then rest a minute. Increase the poundage for your speed-rep set and pump it for 60 seconds.

You should have at least six months' experience lifting weights before you attempt this advanced concept. If you are a very advanced lifter, you may choose to do a second exercise for the same body part. Do that one as you normally do: medium pace, eight to ten reps, and three to four sets. Most likely, though, you'll find that one exercise is plenty.

At first you might want to do speed reps for just one body part. This gives you the opportunity to see how the exercise feels and what adjustments need to be made. In time, you might want to add a second speed set for another body part and eventually do a speed set for each major muscle group.

Let's say that after six weeks you have reached a point where you just can't squeeze another rep out of your 60-second set. This means that you have reached a plateau and it's time to switch to another concept for that body part. You may want to do regular sets and reps for a few weeks, or you might want to try the opposite of speed reps and do extremely slow reps.

Some lifters change concepts each workout. For example, on Mondays they do speed reps; Wednesdays they do slow reps; Fridays they do normal reps and sets. The idea is to keep the muscles surprised so that they are forced to adjust. Once again, this is just for advanced weight trainees.

Speed reps are a tough way to train. You may not want to do them on a regular basis but rather use them only once or twice a year to force your muscles out of a rut and get you back into the groove of developing power. Experiment to see what works best for you.

Free tip: Do not forcefully lock out your joints. Stop each rep just short of lockout and live to exercise for many years to come.

Dead Stops

In Chapter 12, I describe "dead stops" as an excellent way to bench press to develop power in all straight-line punches. However, they are also productive in other weight-resistance exercises. The concept is to stop the momentum of a movement for two seconds at the bottom of a repetition and then, using pure power, ram the weight upward.

For example, when performing a standing military press, you would lower the weight to your shoulders, pause for two seconds, and then press it upward. A squat is held for two seconds in the squatting position and then powered up to the standing position. Any type of seated or lying pressing exercise for the triceps is held for two seconds in the down position before driving the weight upward. Think of exercises that require the weight to be pushed away after the two-second pause as approximating the outward motion of a straight-line kick and punch.

When doing pulling exercises, however, the weight is not pushed away afterward but, rather, resisted and controlled as gravity pulls it back to its starting position. When doing back exercises with the lat bar, for example, pull the bar to your chest, hold for two seconds, then slowly extend your arms as you return the weight to the beginning position. When doing arm curls, it is best to use cables, pulleys, or machines that provide constant tension throughout the movement. Hold for two seconds in the contracted position and then resist gravity as you slowly lower the weight.

When doing dead stops, hold the bar at the down position for a two-second count and then explode the weight upward.

Using dead stops for pulling movements will increase your power in grappling techniques.

HOW MANY REPS SHOULD YOU DO?

There is a lot of confusion among beginners as to how many repetitions to do to get bulk, power, and definition and to improve athletic performance. It's even hard to find two veteran lifters to agree on which method is ideal. So the best I can do here is offer you some generalities and suggest, as I do all the way through this text, that you experiment to see what works best for you.

First let's define the terms. A *low-rep set* is one to six reps, a *medium-rep set* is six to 12, and a *high-rep set* is 12 reps and beyond.

High reps are generally thought to develop definition, which they will if the diet is restricted. If the diet is normal, high reps will actually put on size—though it deflates quickly when high-rep exercise is stopped—but do little for power and strength.

Low-rep exercise will develop strength and power. But (isn't there always a "but" when something is too good?) you can easily burn yourself out physically and mentally, and there is a higher risk of injury.

Medium-rep training is the happy middle ground between low- and high-rep exercise. Use medium reps most of the time, but know that if you do too many medium-rep training sessions, you will cease to progress.

Then what the hell am I suppose to do, you ask? First, calm down. It's not that bad. Here is a way to train that will help you reach your goal of more powerful punches, kicks and blocks. After you have been training for six months with a basic, medium-rep routine, switch to the following procedure. Switch to a low-rep, heavier routine for four weeks. Then go back to medium rep training for four weeks, even if you feel like you want to do more weeks of low reps.

If you are interested in putting on muscle size, do four weeks of high-rep exercises every third month. If you don't care about size, just alternate between four weeks of medium reps and four weeks of low reps, and do high reps for a month two or three times a year when you feel you need to break up the monotony and give your muscles a little shock.

WAYS TO SCHEDULE YOUR WORKOUTS

Your work, school, and workouts all take a tremendous toll on your energy reserves. Besides getting sufficient sleep and eating healthy foods, the way in which you schedule your workouts is all important for keeping your energy at its highest. Earlier we discussed how Bruce Lee scheduled his martial arts and weight-lifting workout so he could get the most out of each. Here are some other ideas you can draw on as a basis for your workouts.

Split Routine

The majority of top body builders follow a concept called *split routine*, a method of dividing training so that not only do they conserve energy but they are also able to work each body part harder. Will this work for a martial artist who wants to supplement his training with weights? Yes, but you have got to experiment and get creative.

Here are a few split routines commonly used in weight training. Examine them and determine how your martial art practice can fit in.

Four-Day Split

The first two routines listed here are called *push* and *pull*. A pushing exercise is one that primarily uses the triceps, such as specific triceps exercises, shoulder presses, and bench presses. Pulling exercises mostly use the biceps, such as specific biceps exercises and most back work. Neck, abdominals, forearms, and legs are split between the two days since they are not considered pushing or pulling exercises.

Method 1

Monday	Perform all pushing exercises
Tuesday	Perform all pulling exercises
Wednesday	Rest
Thursday	Perform the same pushing exercises as on Monday
Friday	Perform the same pulling exercises as on Tuesday
Saturday	Rest
Sunday	Rest

Method 2

Monday	Perform all pushing exercises
Tuesday	Perform all pulling exercises
Wednesday	Perform same pushing exercises as on Monday

Thursday	Perform same pulling exercises as on Tuesday
Friday	Rest
Saturday	Rest
Sunday	Rest

Method 3

In this variation of the split routine, use any variations of the above two weekly schedules you like. Your routine is split by doing all upper body exercises on one day and all lower body exercises the next.

Method 4

This approach is rare, but it might be worth considering. Choose one of the first two scheduling methods, but split your workout by performing all the major muscle groups (chest, back, and legs) the first day and then do all the smaller muscle groups (arms, shoulders, neck, calves, and forearms) the next.

Whole-Body Routines

Here are two ways to schedule whole-body workouts:

Thrice Weekly Workout

This is a classic way to schedule your weight training, though it's considered a little antiquated today. It involves training the entire body each workout, normally on Monday, Wednesday, and Friday.

If you choose this whole-body approach, remember that you shouldn't lift hard and heavy every workout. Hard training requires more time to recuperate than you get on the three-day-a-week routine. You might consider medium-intensity workouts on Monday and Wednesday and a hard workout on Friday. A better plan yet for training the entire body at one time might be the twice-weekly routine.

Twice Weekly Workout

This method is a popular way for martial artists to incorporate weight training with their martial art goals. I have used this one for years and still make gains on it. I do it this way.

I train hard in martial arts on Monday and Wednesday and medium hard on Saturday. I lift weights on Tuesday, but only at three-quarter intensity since I trained on Monday for two hours and will train again on Wednesday. On Friday I lift hard and heavy because I had a rest day on Thursday and will have just a medium martial art workout on Saturday.

Whether you choose one of the split routines or the whole-body three- or two-day plan, the trick is to determine how to fit it into your martial art training schedule.

Free tip: If you are forced to lift on the same day you practice your art, lift afterward because weight training tightens your muscles. If you can only lift before your martial art training, stretch your entire body for at least 15 minutes before you do your lifting.

Whatever method you use to combine your lifting and fighting art, it's important to schedule one day or, preferably, two days a week to rest. Keep in mind that hard workouts mandate 48 hours of recovery. You may get by with resting only one day between workouts for a while, but your body will start letting you know it needs rest. Your progress will slow or stop completely, and your injury rate will accelerate.

It's worth repeating: no matter what method you choose to combine your fighting art with your weight training, you must include rest days in your schedule. One is good; two are better.

CHAPTER FIVE

PLYOMETRICS

Developed by the Russians in the early 1960s, plyometric exercise is a specialized method of training that builds explosive power quickly. It's a relatively unusual way of exercising that dramatically taxes muscles and does so with some inherent risk of injury. But with caution and experimentation, you may find plyometric exercise fun because it's different and result oriented.

Plyometrics is not one specific exercise, but rather a method of doing familiar exercises plyometrically. You probably have done exercises that fit the criteria, but didn't know you were doing them in this special way.

A plyometric exercise is based on how your muscles react when weight is suddenly thrust upon them. For example, say someone was to hand you a paper bag and tell you that it was full of feathers. But when you reach out to take it, you are surprised to find it contains a 25-pound barbell plate. Your biceps suddenly stretch from the surprise overload and then reflexively contract to recover so as not to drop the plate.

This reflex-recovery action is capable of generating tremendous force, much more than you can generate by conscious effort. But by doing plyometric movements systematically—two or three times a week with progressive increases in weight or repetition—you will increase your eccentric strength and power. The eccentric portion of a movement is when the muscle lengthens as it contracts, such as the up motion of a bench press repetition or the outward motion of a punch, backfist, or front kick. Eccentric muscle contraction is stronger than concentric, as when the muscle shortens when curling a barbell upward. Let's get technical for just a moment.

Inside each muscle fiber is something called the *muscle spindle*, which consists of muscle protein, fluid, and nerve receptors. Inside this is another type of muscle fiber called *intrafusal*, which doesn't have the normal contracting capabilities of other muscles. The fibers are covered with nerve cells that carry information from the muscle to the central nervous system. So when that 25-pound barbell plate is dropped unexpectedly into your hand and the muscle is suddenly stretched, the intrafusal fibers stimulate these muscle cells and speed relay messages to the central nervous system. Then the central nervous system sparks a muscle reflex action that creates a tremendous contraction, or stretch reflex. This is a protective mechanism that delivers explosive force to resist sudden stress on the muscles.

As a martial artist, you can use this protective mechanism to develop tremendous power in your punches and kicks. By modifying certain exercises, you can trigger this reflex action to activate deep muscle fibers more quickly and strongly than when exercising in a conventional manner.

To make an exercise plyometric, the muscle stretch must be done quickly. Speed of the overload is more important than how far the muscle is stretched. If the muscle is stretched slowly, as with regularly performed exercises, the stretch reflex doesn't activate. In other words, to stimulate your muscles' reflexive power, the stretch must happen fast.

Plyometric training develops nerve patterns that increase the muscles' ability to switch from eccentric to concentric with great speed. It trains the muscles to resist or overcome a sudden overload and then counters it with force.

Plyometric training also takes advantage of a muscle phenomenon called *anticipatory contraction*, an action that occurs when your muscles anticipate a sudden overload. This anticipation tenses the muscles and allows them to change energy into explosive power quickly. Anticipation cannot be forced; it must happen naturally or it may not happen at all. By training plyometrically, you will develop your ability to anticipate, or pre-tense your muscles prior to the overload. The end result is that you will be able to come out of the stretch with greater speed and power.

Both conventional weight training and plyometric training strive to increase muscle strength, size, and power. Conventional lifting, however, relies on conscious contractions of the muscles, whereas plyometrics rely on reflexes and anticipatory response to develop ultimate power.

There is some controversy surrounding plyometric training. A study performed at the Sports Training Institute based in New York showed that plyometrics may not be needed to supplement regular resistance training. Females who weight-trained with conventional exercises and plyometrics did show improvement in strength and power, but no more than those who trained only conventionally.

Some athletes say that plyometric exercise is too strenuous, that when the muscle overloads so quickly, there is a big potential for injury. Not only is the muscle placed under stress, but so are the tendons, joints, and ligaments.

Plyometrics are indeed strenuous and should therefore be approached with caution and total concentration. With

Begin plyometric jumping in the down position and then leap as high as you can. Drop to the starting position and, without pausing, leap up again.

some plyometric movements, you may not experience the same kind of muscle fatigue as with other weight-resistance exercises. You may not feel a muscle burn or pump. You feel tired the day after, even wiped out, but at the moment you are doing plyometrics it's easy to be fooled into thinking you are not doing enough.

Free tip: If you have bad elbows or bad knees, avoid doing exercises plyometrically. They are not worth the risk.

There are martial artists who believe in the plyometric approach and swear by the results, which leads to the assumption that plyometric exercise has not hurt these fighters. If the exercises don't hurt you, carefully incorporate them into your training and monitor the results. If they start to bother you, stop doing them immediately .

Don't start out with three sets of 10 pushups or five sets of power hops. Instead, start with one set at low intensity, gradually increasing it over two or three weeks until you can safely go at full intensity. Then add another low-intensity set and build on it until you can do that one at full intensity. Then add a third set and build it to full intensity. Use this slow-building process even if you have been lifting weights for several years. Plyometric exercising is new to your muscles and can be a shock if your approach is overzealous. Always use good form. Sloppy form, or form that turns sloppy because of fatigue, will lead to injury.

The plyometric hopping exercises illustrated on page 104 should be done on soft surfaces, such as grass, sawdust, a gym mat, or thick carpet. Cement, asphalt, and gymnasium floors are too hard and may lead to injury. Wear shoes with good support even when doing the exercises on soft surfaces. Don't add weight to the exercises, since plyometrics require you to burst out of the stretch with speed. Added weight will slow you and diminish the effect.

Plyometric exercise requires more rest than conventional exercise. Always remember that you can't move explosively if you are fatigued. Consider resting 10 times longer than it took to do the exercise. So, if you take 10 seconds to pump out your push-ups, you need to rest 100 seconds. This is too long to rest in most bodybuilding circles, but then you are training to develop explosive muscles, not just the showy kind.

Rest for five minutes between exercises, even if you are doing two different ones for the same muscle group, such as two for punching power.

You will find plyometric variations clearly labeled throughout this book. Although I suggest three sets of 10 reps with most of them, understand that that is an ultimate objective, not a starting point—even if you are advanced.

CHAPTER SIX

ISOMETRICS

S ince isometric exercises don't require special equipment, you can do them just about anywhere. They can be done in conjunction with other exercises or by themselves. They will keep your muscles toned and strong when you are unable to get to a gym, and, as mentioned earlier, they will help you recuperate from an injury.

Although I have listed isometric exercises here, you can use your imagination to create others to strengthen any movement you want. I usually break a movement into three parts, although there is nothing keeping you from breaking it into five or even 10 parts.

UPPER-BODY TECHNIQUES

Let's look at isometric exercises you can do against a wall.

Backfist

Face a wall in a right-leg-forward fighting stance. Stand close enough so that you can place your index and middle knuckles against the wall, with your arm positioned as if you were just beginning to extend the strike. Press your knuckles as hard as you can against the wall for six seconds and then relax your arm for 20 seconds. On the second set, step back a little and extend your arm halfway out, again placing your knuckles against the wall. Press as hard as you can for six seconds and then relax for 20 seconds. The final set is to extend your arm all the way out but just short of locking your elbow. Again press your knuckles against the wall and press hard for six seconds. Repeat this procedure with both arms.

Sometimes I repeat the exercise five to 10 times in one position before I move on to the next. Other times, I go through all three positions one time, then start over at the first stage and go through all three again, repeating this for five to 10 cycles.

In all three of these positions, or how ever many you choose

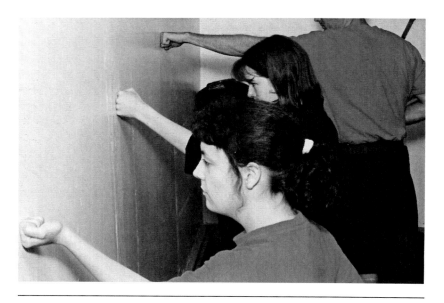

Hold each punch position for six seconds, with a 20-second rest in between.

to do, it's important to consciously feel your knuckles, wrist, triceps, shoulder, back, waist, and legs. Consciously extend your energy, not just to the wall's surface, but beyond it.

Reverse Punch

Stand close to a wall in a left-leg-forward fighting stance and extend your right arm one third of the way out, palm side up, as if just starting to punch. Press your middle and index knuckles against the wall and push hard for six seconds. To do the second stage, step back far enough so you can extend your arm halfway out, fist rotated so that the thumb side is up, and press your knuckles against the wall. Press hard for six seconds. For the third stage, step back so you can touch the wall with a fully extended arm just short of total lockout. Press your knuckles against the wall and press as hard as you can for six seconds.

As with the backfist, you should press for only six seconds and then rest for twenty. You may precede through all three stages and then do all three again. Or you may do one stage five to 10 times, the second stage five to 10 times, and then the third.

Roundhouse or Hook Punch

Stand in front of a door facing and place your right fist against the wall. Sidestep to the left far enough so that your arm is positioned as if you were just starting the punch, and then push for six seconds. To work the middle stage, sidestep a little more to your right to position your arm midway into the punch and push for six seconds. Sidestep again, positioning your fist even with your solar plexus, and push for six seconds.

To make the exercise a little harder, brace yourself against the wall with your other hand so that you can apply some counterresistance. This enables you to push harder and bring more muscles into the action, primarily those of the upper chest.

Take a look at some of your other hand techniques to

determine how you can best incorporate isometric training into the track of the movement. Do at least three sections, the beginning to strengthen the takeoff, the middle to add power to the building phase, and the end position so that the technique will hit with optimum impact.

These are just a few exercises you can do using a wall. Experiment to find others that are applicable to your needs. Now, let's look at some exercises you can do when resisting with your own muscles.

Sweep Blocks and Circular Strikes

This isometric exercise will put power into your sweep blocks and all circular strikes, such as roundhouse punches, ridge hands, chops, slaps, and claws.

Place the palms of your hands together as if praying and position them about six inches away from your right shoulder. Think of your left hand as an immovable wall that your right hand is going to push against. Press your right palm hard for six seconds, then rest for 20. Move both hands over to the left about four inches, still six inches away from your upper torso. Press for six seconds and rest for 20. Move your hands over about four inches and continue the procedure until you have done a final set in front of your left shoulder. Now, use your left hand to do the pushing and do the same procedure back across your chest to the right.

Do about six positions on each trip across your chest. One trip in each direction is enough. This set is primarily for strengthening your sweep block since the set is executed close to your body. You can use the same motion to develop power in your circular blows, such as roundhouse, ridge hand, chops, and slaps, but you will need to extend your hands farther out from your torso. You can push with your fist or any hand configuration and proceed with the exercise as you did with the sweep block.

Backfist

Position your right backfist about two inches away from

your chin and place your left palm in front of your backfist. Press your backfist against your immovable palm for six seconds. If this hurts your elbow at this close range, don't push as hard as you do in the other stages. Rest for 20 seconds; then extend your backfist about six inches and press again for six seconds. Repeat this procedure until your backfist is fully extended. One trip out with each arm should be sufficient, but if you feel like you want to do two, go ahead.

Uppercut

Resisting your uppercut fist can be done basically the same way as you did with the backfist, except that you start this exercise with your right fist along your side. Use your left palm to resist the punch as you proceed through the six 6-second stages to full extension.

Straight Punches

Straight punches are executed the same way as uppercuts except that the punch goes straight out rather than up. Position the punching hand along your side and resist with your opposite hand. Again, use six 6-second stages and work your way out to full extension.

LEGS

Balancing on one leg makes standing-leg isometric exercise difficult, if not impossible. I don't know any good ones for kicks using a wall or your own muscles as resistance. But here are a few other methods that, although not as task specific as the isometrics for the punches, will nonetheless add power to your kicks and strength to your stances.

Knee Isometrics

This was taught to me by a physical therapist as part of my recuperation after blowing my kneecap in a sparring match. It not only helped to stabilize the joint and get my strength back, it added muscle around the knee to safe-

Vary the height of your horse stance for each set and alternate pressing your knee inward and then outward against your hands for six seconds.

guard the joint against any surprise movements. If your knees are already healthy, the added muscle around the knees will increase your snapping power.

Sit in a chair and slip your foot under a heavy coffee table, sofa, or any immovable object. Sit close enough so that your shin is vertical and push against the object for six seconds and then rest for 20. Scoot your chair back a few inches so that your lower leg extends at a slight angle and again contract your muscles for six seconds. Continue scooting back until your leg is fully locked out. Do an additional two or three sets at full extension to work this critical position thoroughly. Break the exercise into three to six stages and go through them two or three times.

Horse Stance Leg Push
Assume the horse stance and place your hands on the

outside of your knees. As you resist with your hands, push outward with your knees for six seconds. Rest for 20 seconds and repeat for six sets. To work the muscles on the inside of the thighs, place your hands on the insides of your knees. As you resist with your hands, press inward with your knees. Rest for 20 seconds and repeat for six sets.

I have found that I completely work the muscles at one height in the horse stance, but if you want to do them in varying heights, go ahead. You are not going to hurt anything.

Never hold your breath when doing isometrics. Exhale slowly as you push or pull for your six seconds and use the 20-second rest period to recapture your breath.

Although isometrics won't stiffen your muscles to the same extent that isotonic exercises do, it's still a good idea to spend a few minutes stretching afterward.

CHAPTER SEVEN

DYNAMIC TENSION

Have you ever watched a house cat stretch? Little Fifi can practically double her length as she reaches with her rear legs north and her front legs south. Her little legs vibrate as she tenses every muscle from whisker to tail.

Have you ever wondered how Fifi can jump from the floor to the top of your fireplace mantel? She doesn't begin to look like Arnold Schwarzenegger, yet she can jump six or seven times her own height. Can you?

Unless Fifi is secretly pumping iron out in the garage, her tremendous strength can be attributed to the way she exercises by stretching and tensing her muscles continually. Actually, Fifi isn't the only creature that exercises this way: dogs do it, as do big jungle cats, horses, and birds. It's even possible the powerful ant might do it, but who would know?

You can do it, too. "It" is called *dynamic tension*. It can be hard and energy depleting, but you will reap the benefits of greater body awareness, muscle control, and power. On a health note, some advocates believe dynamic tension helps to keep your veins and arteries cholesterol free. You get all this, plus you are able to exercise the exact muscles you want to make stronger.

The basis of dynamic tension is that you pit your own muscles against your own muscles. It's called dynamic because there is movement, as opposed to isometric tension in which there is none. There are no barbells or dumbbells to contend with and no machines to oil. The chance of your getting injured is greatly reduced because you have control over the intensity of the exercise. If a movement is too difficult, you simply reduce the applied tension. With a barbell, however, the tendency is to continue the difficult exercise, risking a strain or pull.

As with any exercise, it's imperative that your mind be focused on each repetition. If you have had trouble concentrating on your exercises, you may find that it's easier to stay mentally in tune with your muscles when doing dynamic tension. As opposed to having an inanimate object responsible for your muscle action, your own body creates the tension, making it easier to concentrate on the task.

Put your mind into the muscles you are working; visualize what is happening under your skin. See and feel the muscles contract harder and harder; see and feel them relax. In time, visualizing the action will become easier and easier as you discover greater control over all of your muscles.

As when doing any exercise that involves intense muscle tension, proper breathing is essential. Holding your breath is not only unhealthy, it could be dangerous. To breathe correctly, simply exhale when pushing and inhale when retracting your limb.

Where and when you train is up to you. Since dynamic tension exercises don't require equipment, you can do them any way and anywhere you want. Some of the more subtle movements can even be done in public, such as in a movie theater or grocery line. You can do some of them first thing in the morning, even before you get out of bed, and you can do a few of them in your bathroom at night before you hit the shower.

I like to do two or three dynamic tension exercises in my martial art class and two or three on opposite days when I lift weights. Experiment to see where they fit into your training.

Here is how you apply dynamic tension to three standard blocks.

SWEEP BLOCK

Stand in a natural stance or lower yourself into a horse stance if you want to work your legs at the same time.

The student on the right slowly and with dynamic tension sweeps both hands across his body until they cross. The other student slowly resists the sweep motion with her fist.

Keeping your elbows at your sides, raise your forearms so that they are at a 45-degree angle in front of you, fingertips as high as your shoulders, open palms facing each other.

Tense your hands, arms, shoulders, and chest as you slowly move your hands toward the center of your body in a sweeping motion. Your hands pass each other and stop when they are about 10 inches apart. Alternate which hand is in front. Relax at the conclusion of the sweep and move your hands back to the starting point.

Do five reps to complete one set. On the first four, let your hands pass each other as described. On the fifth rep, bring your palms together, pressing hard for six seconds to add an isometric technique to the exercise.

For a variation, sweep one hand across your body as you apply resistance with your opposite hand. Start with your right hand, resisting it with your left fist or open hand as you sweep across the front of your body. Make sure the tension is constant and the sweep is smooth.

Vary the heights. Sweep at face height for one set and do a second set at abdominal height and one at belt height.

RISING BLOCK

The rising block is a common defense move in most fighting styles. Some practitioners execute the block close to the forehead; others, such as my style, extend it farther away. It's important that you do this exercise the way you do your block.

Stand naturally, use the horse stance, or assume the fighting posture of your choice. Tense all the muscles in your left hand, forearm, upper arm, shoulder, and neck as you slowly execute a left rising block. At the end of the movement, reduce the tension in your left arm as you slowly retract it, and put all the tension in your right arm as it slowly ascends into the block. Your arms should cross in front of your chest. Do three sets of six reps.

For a variation, use your opposite hand to apply resistance to the rising block. Grasp your right wrist with your left and resist your arm as it rises into the block. Do the movement smoothly.

DOWNWARD BLOCK

Think of this block as making a halfcircle in front of your lower torso. Use a natural, horse, or other fighting stance.

Begin with your fists held in front of your chin. Tense your left fist, forearm, upper arm, shoulder, neck, and upper body as you slowly lower your arm downward to the left. Stop your fist in front of your leg without locking your elbow. As you reduce some of the tension in your left arm and begin to retract it on the same path on which it descended, tense your right arm and slowly lower it into the block. Your arms will cross at about belt height. Do three sets of six reps.

A variation is to resist the downward circle motion with your opposite hand. Grasp your right wrist with your left hand and apply resistance as your arm arcs downward.

Although I suggest here that you reduce the tension in the blocking arm as it is retracted, you may choose to relax your arms completely or maintain maximum tension in them. You may find that retracting without tension helps teach you to relax the muscles after the block, enhancing your ability to snap the arm back quickly. On the other hand, you may want to maintain the tension so that you develop the muscles needed to move the arm in the opposite direction. I'm like a good politician and take the middle ground, relaxing a little and maintaining a little tension. Experiment to see which you like.

The above blocks are standard in most fighting styles. The rising block covers the upper quadrant, the sweep covers the middle (it can also be used to block the upper quadrant), and the downward block covers the lower section. If your style uses different blocks, simply apply dynamic tension to them as just described.

Begin the downward dynamic tension block with both fists held under your chin (left). Then slowly and with dynamic tension, lower your left block (center). A variation is to resist the block with your opposite hand.

Let's see how you can use dynamic tension to develop powerful hand blows. As with blocking movements, you may retract these without tension, with medium tension, or with maximum tension.

BACKFIST

Using dynamic tension to strengthen the backfist also works the muscles used in grabbing and pulling.

Assume the horse stance and place your left palm on your solar plexus and your right fist on top of your left hand. Keep your palm on your solar plexus and slowly extend your right backfist, maintaining dynamic tension in your fist, forearm, upper arm, shoulder, chest, and abdomen. Extend the backfist all the way out and then slowly and dynamically return it to your solar plexus.

Relax for a moment and then repeat. Do three sets of six reps with each fist.

A variation is to resist the backfist motion with your opposite hand. Place the back of your right fist into your left palm and resist as you slowly move the backfist outward. If you want resistance on the retraction, simply move your left palm around to the other side of your fist to resist its return.

The student on the left executes a backfist with dynamic force while yours truly uses the right hand to resist the left backfist.

STRAIGHT PUNCHING

This exercise stimulates all the muscles involved in the basic punches, such as reverse, straight, jab, and all other varieties of straight-line hand attacks. Use whatever stance you want, although the horse stance lines up your body perfectly for this exercise.

Begin with both fists at your hips. Tense the muscles of your hand, forearms, upper arms, shoulder, neck, chest, and abdominals as you slowly extend your right arm, rotating your fist as you go. Maintain tension as you reach the point of full extension and then begin to extend your left fist as

your right one re-
tracts. Your fists will
pass at the halfway
point. Do three sets
of six reps.

A variation is to
resist your punch
with the opposite
hand. Place your left
palm in front of your
right fist and resist
the outward trajec-
tory of the punch.

ROUNDHOUSE
PUNCH

This is a great
exercise for develop-
ing power in the
roundhouse punch.
Not only does it
work the arms, but
it stimulates the
specific waist mus-
cles necessary to ac-
centuate the punch's
circular direction of
force.

The student on the left executes a dynamic tension
reverse punch, and I resist mine with my opposite hand.

Stand in a natural stance with your right fist in your left
palm and position both in front of the right side of your chest.
As you resist with your left palm, push with your right fist
across your body until you have reached the far left. At that
point, open your right hand and place your left fist in the right
palm and push across your chest to the opposite side. One trip
to the left and one trip to the right count as one rep. Be sure
to turn your waist about a quarter of a turn as you complete

each punch. Do three sets of five to 10 reps.

FINGER STRENGTHENING FOR CLAWING AND GRABBING

This is a great exercise for strengthening your fingers, hands, wrists, and forearms to enable you to grab an opponent more powerfully.

Stand in a natural stance and press your palms together in front of you, all fingers touching. It's rather like a praying position but with the fingers spread as wide as possible. Now, apply pressure with your fingertips against each other as your palms slowly separate. Continue to

You can supply your own resistance for the roundhouse punch by pushing against it with your open palm as it slowly moves across the front of your body.

apply finger pressure until your palms are as far apart as they can go and then slowly move your palms back together until they are touching. Imagine a spider doing push-ups on a mirror. Relax for a moment and repeat. Do three sets of five reps.

PUMP UP YOUR TOES

Yes, it's possible to strengthen your toes with dynamic

tension. Strong toes will help you maintain a strong stance, give you greater control to curl them back when kicking, and help you absorb the impact of your powerful kicks. The exercises are easy—you can even do them while watching TV.

Toe Waving

While this exercise is basically a warm-up for the dynamic tension toe exercises that follow, it will also develop control, speed, flexibility, and strength in the toe joint. You can work both feet at the same time or one at a time.

Position your feet so that they are resting on their heels. Now, wave all your toes up and down as fast as you can. Don't wiggle them in an irregular fashion, but rather move all of them down and back as if waving. Do three 30-second sets.

Toe-Resistance Exercises

Sit in a chair, bend forward, and place your hands against your toes. Push down as you draw your toes up against the resistance. This is dynamic tension, not an isometric, so let your toes win. Do three sets of 10 reps.

Toe Curls

The last exercise works the tops of the toes, but this one works the muscles underneath them. Sit in a chair and place your bare feet on the front edge of a large bath towel. Use all 10 toes to bunch the towel, drawing its entire length toward you. Repeat until tired.

CHAPTER EIGHT

DEVELOPING A POWERFUL NECK

Say you're in a clinch with your attacker and he has tied your arms up so that you are unable to punch, elbow, or forearm strike. But you see a clear path between your head and your attacker's upper chest. You have trained your neck muscles to be fast and strong, so you snap your head forward, ramming your forehead into the exposed and sensitive portion of the attacker's upper chest. Would this have been an effective blow if your head had been supported by a poorly conditioned neck? No.

A strong neck is needed when grappling. Because most fights end up on the floor, a strong neck may be a deciding factor in whether you get out of a hold or from under a pin. Ask any wrestler how important the so-called wrestler's bridge is.

A strong neck is also an asset when getting hit in the head with a hard punch or kick. If you have a weak neck, your head is going to snap back and your brain is going to slam into your skull like a melon thrown against a wall. This is known as a concussion, and the last thing you will be aware of before you hit the floor is Tweety Bird whistling a little song. A strong neck will go a long way toward minimizing the shock and whiplash effect of a hard blow to the head.

Visually, a muscular neck is more impressive than a neck that looks like a pencil holding up a fat eraser. If you were a bully, would you pick on a person whose thick muscular neck implies that there is a powerful body below that just might fight back? Or would you choose a person who looks like an easy mark because of his scrawny, weak neck?

For all these reasons and more, it's important to include neck exercises in your routine. It doesn't take a lot to strengthen it, and the rewards are invaluable. Let's take a look at just a few of the many exercises you can do.

PARTNER ASSIST

Get down on your hands and knees as your training partner stands in front of you. To exercise the back of your neck, he places his hands on the back of your head and applies resistance as you slowly lift your head and as you lower it. Your partner should keep the resistance constant throughout the full range of movement. Do three sets of 10 reps.

To work the front of your neck, lie on your back as your partner positions himself behind your head. As he applies steady pressure on your forehead, slowly lift your head. Do three sets of 10 reps.

To work the sides, lie on your side as your partner positions himself behind you. As he applies hand pressure against your head, slowly lift it up and slowly lower it. After you have completed three sets of 10 reps, turn over and do the same thing for the other side of your neck.

Caution: It's easy to overextend your neck muscles, so be careful of extending your head too far back or forward.

BARBELL PLATE RESISTANCE

This exercise looks a little odd but it works, and that's what counts. Lie on a bench so that the back of your head extends over the edge. Place a folded towel on your forehead and a barbell plate on the towel. The towel is for comfort and so you won't leave an imprint of the plate's little center circle on your forehead.

Use your fingertips to keep the plate from falling off as you lower and raise your head. Keep your movements smooth and in a straight line to prevent the sudden overloading of one of your small neck muscles.

Next, lie on your left side with your head over the bench's edge and place the towel and plate on the right side of your head. Hold the plate in place with your right hand as you move your head up and down. Repeat on the other side.

Here I use two 25-pound plates for resistance as I raise and lower my head over the end of a bench.

To work the muscles on the back of the neck, lie on your stomach with your head extended over the bench. Place the towel and plate on the back of your head (this is awkward at best) and hold them in place as you move your head up and down.

Choose a weight for all of these exercises that allows you to do 10 to 12 reps for three sets on each side.

CHAPTER NINE

PUSH-UPS

f push-ups increased muscle size, I would have completed army basic training with 42-inch arms. Every time I screwed up, the drill sergeant would scream at me, "Christensen, give me 50 push-ups!" It was always 50 or 75, never just five or 10. Sometimes I had to do them two or three times in one hour. By the time I graduated from basic and advanced training, I was convinced I had done at least one push-up for every star in the sky.

A PERSONAL PREJUDICE

Instructors, don't discipline your students by making them do push-ups. The old "Give me 10!" has probably turned more people off exercise, especially young people, than any other one thing. If you want your students to benefit from exercise, why in the world would you use it as punishment? If your style of teaching is to punish your students for errors and infractions (that's another subject of debate), choose something other than exercise.

OK, I feel better now.

If, for some odd reason, you were unable to do any other exercise except push-ups, you wouldn't be that bad off. Although they only mildly stimulate the biceps muscles, they are excellent for conditioning and strengthening the shoulders, chest, back, upper arms, stomach, neck, wrists, and hands.

If you are interested in gaining muscle size in the upper arms, you may or may not be able to do so with push-ups. I never have, even when I was doing zillions of them for my country. I did get in condition, and I did get to the point where I could whip off a hundred without much effort, but my arms never looked like Arnold Schwarzenneger's.

There are, however, many variations of the push-up movement, and lots of routines that just might increase muscle size. So if free-hand exercises are the only exercises you can do, and you want to increase your muscle size as well as your power, explore the variety of ways to do the common push-up.

But will push-ups help your karate? Definitely. The exercise duplicates the motion of the punch—jab, straight, reverse—working the exact muscles needed to deliver a powerful blow.

Do females have to do push-ups differently than men? No, that's an old wives' tale. If a female is way out of shape and lacks upper-body strength, she may want to start out doing them on her knees, but the same is true for any man who is out of condition. If you have to start out that way, that's fine. But your immediate goal is to do them off your knees, and then progress to the more difficult variations.

Let's take a look at a few variations of the push-up and see how it can be used to put power in your punches.

PAUSE PUSH-UP

Assume the regular push-up position, hands about shoulder-width apart, and your legs spread as far as possible to stretch your back, stomach, and groin area. Lower yourself until you are about two inches from the floor and hold the position for 30 seconds. Push yourself back up to the starting position, hold for five seconds, and do another rep.

If these are hard for you, do only five reps, rest a moment, and do another five. Work up to three sets of 10 reps.

FOREARM PUSH-UP

This is a great triceps pumper; three sets of eight will inflate your arms like balloons.

A word of caution: If you have problem elbows—pain, clicking, etc.—this variation might aggravate the problem. If so, skip it.

Assume the standard push-up position but with your forearms rather than your palms on the floor. To begin the movement, press your palms down with enough force to lift your forearms off the floor. Continue pressing until they are vertical and then reverse the motion by slowly lowering your elbows back to the floor. Continue in this fashion until you have completed one set.

ONE-ARM PUSH-UP

These have been around for a long time, but actors Sylvester Stallone in the movie *Rocky* and Jack Palance at the 1993 Academy Awards ceremony made them a household word.

One-arm push-ups can put quite a bit of stress on the elbow joint and all the support parts that make the joint function, so you should do these only after your triceps and elbows have been thoroughly warmed up from other exercises. Don't do them at all if you have elbow problems.

Begin the forearm push-ups on your forearms (left) and slowly press up until your arms are straight. Lower slowly back onto your forearms and repeat.

Assume the standard two-hand push-up position, then twist your upper body so that it's positioned over your right arm. Chamber your left fist at your hip. Lower yourself down as far as you can go comfortably and then push back up.

Do them on the palm of your hand until you get the hang of them and then on your knuckles to strengthen your hands and wrists. Eventually you may want to try them just on your thumb and index finger.

RIB-RUBBING PUSH-UP

Assume the push-up position, hands directly under your shoulders. Keep your elbows tucked in snugly against your sides so that the up-and-down motion simulates the same motion as in straight and reverse punching. Keep your back straight and your chin up.

To develop the entire range of the punch, place your hands on two 2-inch-high blocks so that your body descends farther than when your hands are on the floor. When you have lowered yourself as far as you can go, your hands will be about halfway back along your sides. Then as you push yourself up, your muscles (in particular, your punching muscles) will be worked through the entire range of the punch.

SPADE PUSH-UP

This position stimulates the outer triceps head. Assume the push-up position with the tips of your index fingers and thumbs touching. The space between your fingers will look like a spade. Spread your legs to get a good stretch in your chest and groin. Lower yourself until your chest just touches the floor and then push up until your arms are straight. Hold the upright position for 10 to 15 seconds; then lower yourself again. Do three sets of 10 to 15 reps.

PLYOMETRIC PUSH-UP

This requires a powerful thrust to propel you off the floor, enhancing your ability to explode with the muscles of your arms, shoulders, chest, and back. This shouldn't be confused with the type of push-up where you clap your hands in the air. The plyometric variation is harder because you don't go up as far and you drop down farther, all of which make the action faster. Begin in a standard push-up position with your chest and legs touching the floor and then push up so forcefully that your hands come off the floor. Keep your arms bent and your hands even with your chest as you drop back to the floor; then explode right back up again. This exercise doesn't work the full range of motion, which is OK.

Think of this as bouncing off your hands by using a powerful upward motion on each rep. The instant your hands hit the floor, thrust upward with speed and explosive power; make it your goal to touch the floor for as short a time as possible.

Spade push-ups (left) are done by forming the shape of a spade with your fingers. Fingertip push-ups are done by turning the hands toward each other.

You may not catch on to the rhythm of this variation right away. Plyometric pushups are extremely hard on your muscles, so make sure you are thoroughly warmed up before you do them. If they are too difficult, start out with your knees on the floor. Do three sets of 10 reps.

FINGERTIPS-TOUCHING PUSH-UPS

Assume the push-up position. With your palms on the floor, turn your fingers inward so that the fingertips of each hand touch. This places some stress on your wrists but mostly on the outer head of the triceps, the portion of the muscle involved in extending the backfist and driving the straight punch. Three sets of 10 should do.

Start the plyometric push-up in the down position, chest and nose touching the floor. Explode up just until your hands leave the floor. Keep your arms bent as you drop back to the starting position and then explode up again.

HANDSTAND PUSH-UPS

You will get a rush from these—a rush of blood to your head. Handstand push-ups take a bit of practice, but they are worth the effort. It's easiest to do them against a wall or have a training partner hold your feet. If you are a gymnast, you can probably do them in the center of a room without support.

Lower yourself as far as you can and then push yourself back up. If at first you can only dip a little, that's OK. Do two or three sets of six reps lowering yourself just a short way. But as your strength increases, progressively lower yourself farther and farther, beginning with one set, then a second set, and then all three. Strive to go all the way down.

• • •

There are many ways to do push-ups. One time, I was teaching a class of 35 students and asked each one of them to come up with a different variation—and they did. Use your imagination and you will discover all kinds of power-building push-ups. Here are few more that should be self-explanatory:

- Hands-set-wide push-ups
- Feet-on-chair-hands-on-floor push-ups
- Hands-touching push-ups
- Back-of-hands push-ups
- Hop-across-the-floor push-ups
- Slow-reps push-ups
- Fast-reps push-ups
- Lower-slowly-explode-upward push-ups
- Clap-hands-between-each-rep push-ups
- Knuckle push-ups
- Thumbs-only push-ups
- Fingertips push-ups
- Edge-of-hand push-ups
- One-finger push-ups
- Partner-sitting-on-back push-ups

Although all push-ups are good, those that position your arms directly underneath your shoulders and allow you to tuck your elbows tightly against your sides are the most beneficial for developing punching power.

Free tip: If you do your push-ups on the same day you

practice your fighting art, it's best to do them at the end of the class. If you do them at the beginning, say as part of your warm-up, you will be too tired to throw quality punches during the class.

CHAPTER TEN

HIPS AND ABDOMINALS

HIPS

It has been my experience as a teacher that if I don't continually remind students to use their hips in their techniques, correct hip rotation is the first to go. I call it "lazy hips," and I must admit I get it too. So is rotating the hips really necessary?

Here are a couple of tests you can do if you still have any doubts as to their importance in generating power. These are also good exercises to get you mentally and physically in tune with using the hips in virtually all of your techniques.

Elbow Strike

Stand in a forward stance with your left leg in front. Place the little-finger edge of your right hand on the side of a striking pad that is being held by your training partner.

To test the importance of hip rotation, touch your little finger to a striking pad. Then, without turning your hips, strike it with your elbow. Next, touch the pad again as in the photo at right and snap your hips as you deliver the strike.

Now, strike the bag without turning your hips. Repeat the strike a few times so you can get a feel for the extent of your power—or lack of it.

Now, assume the same stance as before, but this time snap your hips forward as you deliver your fast elbow strike. If you do it correctly, you should hit the bag at least twice as hard as you did when you used only your arm power.

Delivering an elbow strike in this fashion is not only just a good way to test the power of the hips, but it's also a viable technique. Say an attacker is literally on top of you, so close that you don't have enough space to deliver a punch. If you have developed snapping power in your hips, you will be able to drive a powerful elbow strike into the attacker's face or body even though the strike will travel only a short distance.

Here is another test.

Palm Strike

Set yourself in a left-leg-forward stance with your right palm six to eight inches away from your partner's hand-held striking pad. Without turning your hips, extend your arm as quickly as you can to strike the pad. Do it several times so that you can evaluate your power.

Now, assume the same stance as before, but this time use your hips to drive your palm into the target. If you do it correctly, you will strike the pad at least twice as hard as when only using arm power.

Hip-Rotation Exercises

I discussed these in detail in *Speed Training*, so I'll just briefly illustrate two of them here. Do them in front of a mirror to ensure your form is correct.

Assume a forward stance, with your left leg in front. Make sure your upper body is angled to the right about one-quarter turn. Place a hand on each hip, with your left elbow forward a quarter turn and your right elbow back a quarter turn.

Now, snap your hips forward. The trick is to use your hips to do the snap and not your arms. The function of your arms is to see that your hips are rotating enough so that your upper body and elbows are forward at the end of the movement. Do three sets of 10 reps on both sides.

In the second exercise, place a pole, *bo*, or broom across your lower back and hold it there with your hands. Angle your upper body away from the mirror one-quarter turn. Snap your hips forward as in the first exercise, making sure that you end up with your upper body facing straight ahead. The angle of the pole will indicate whether you have rotated too little or too far.

The one common element in Chapter 2 was that all systems and styles rely on hip rotation to generate power. Continually train for it and you will reap the benefits.

ABDOMINALS

In a swimsuit, the abdominals are the focal point of the physique and, when flat, tight, and defined, give an overall impression of muscularity and fitness. Whether on a male or female, a well-conditioned midsection denotes good health, vitality, and athletic prowess. On the other hand, abdominal muscles coated with a layer of fat give an overall impression of softness and a lack of fitness, energy, and power.

Consider the martial artist whose overabundant midsection threatens to explode the seams of his uniform top. What does that say about that specific individual, his style, his instructor, and the martial arts in general? What if, heaven forbid, it's the instructor whose belly is shaking like an overflowing bowl of Jell-O?

There is no room in the martial arts for a flabby, mushy gut. When we put on a martial art uniform, we are saying that we study an art of self-defense, a unique endeavor that demands discipline and tremendous mental and physical energy.

Aesthetics aside, optimum performance in the martial arts necessitates a hard, strong body. Not only is it necessary to be physically fit to get the most out of your training, but your fitness level may decide the outcome of a street survival situation.

A strong, conditioned stomach provides many benefits to a fighter, such as better support to the lower back, protection of the internal organs, greater energy, and more powerful punches and kicks.

Think of your abdomen as the seat of your external and internal power. Virtually all offensive and defensive techniques gather their force from the middle of the body. Greater power is generated when the abdominals are sharply contracted as your blow hits its target. Try this: throw two roundhouse kicks at a heavy bag, one without contracting your abdominal muscles at the point of impact and one with contraction. Quite a difference, isn't there? Try the same thing with a backfist, a hammerfist, and a front kick.

It takes time to learn how to contract your abdominals at the exact point of impact. But first you have to have muscle to contract—a logical point perhaps, but one obviously missed by a lot of soft-bellied martial artists. The stronger the midsection muscles, the more power you will be able to bring to your techniques. Additionally, ducking, twisting, dodging, and all your ground-fighting techniques will be more fluid and powerful when your midsection is in shape.

Stay away from old-fashioned sit-ups and straight-leg raises. They do a poor job of stimulating the abdominal muscles, and they can cause lower back problems. Crunches are the only way to go. They work the abs without involving the hips or the leg muscles and minimize risk to the back.

You can work the abs daily if you choose. Although it's not necessary, it does feel good to have tight abs for a while after you train. Working them three or four days a week will give you optimum development for the martial arts.

Numerous books, magazines, and videos cover abdominal

routines in detail, and I encourage you to check them out. My school has used variations of the ab workout below for several years, and while the structure remains constant, the exercises change from time to time to keep the routine fresh. I learned the structure from a guy named Hully Fetico several years ago and wrote an article about it in the July 1985 issue of *Black Belt* magazine. Because of an overwhelming demand for photocopies, it was reprinted in the September 1989 *Black Belt*. The reason it was so popular? It works.

Hully believes in spot reducing, though most trainers do not. I'm not going to argue whether it's possible to reduce fat in just one part of your body, but I do know that Hully's students all had muscular midsections, and my students who train diligently at the routine do also. I also know that even when I have been consuming too many chocolate chip cookies and my weight is higher than normal, I still have a relatively muscular midsection.

Here is how the structure of the routine works. The entire abdominal area will be worked because of the varied placement of your feet. For example, when you point your toes inward, you work one part of your midsection; when you point your knees outward, you work another. You will be doing 10 sets, using 10 different foot positions.

How many repetitions you do depends on your physical condition. Though your goal is to do 20 reps, you will be painfully sore if you start out at 20. If you are out of condition (come on, admit it), start out with five reps per set and add a rep to each set every workout or every other workout. If you are in good shape, begin with 10 reps per set and progressively add one rep to each set every workout.

Do all of the exercises on your back, your head resting on your forearms. *Do not pull your head up with your hands.* This takes stress off your abs and can hurt your neck.

Press your lower back into the floor to reduce the stress on your lower back and increase the stress on your abdominal muscles. Curl yourself up until your shoulders have cleared the floor, a point where your abdominal muscles are fully contracted. Here is the routine my class is doing as of this writing. We always work the hard-to-reach lower abs first for three or four sets and then finish with upper-ab work. Work up to 20 reps in each exercise.

The Postures

1. Extend your right leg and hold your left knee close to your chest.
2. Extend your left leg and hold your right knee close to your chest.
3. Hold your slightly apart and bent legs at a 45-degree angle from the floor.
4. Put your legs together, bend slightly, and hold at 45 degrees from the floor.
5. Put your legs together and pull both knees close to your chest.
6. Hold the bottoms of your feet together and spread your knees.
7. Hold both of your legs straight up.
8. Put your feet together and on the floor; put knees together and bend. Lift your knees to your chest with each upper-body crunch.
9. Begin with your upper body a quarter turn to the right with both knees on the floor.
10. Hold upper body a quarter turn to the left with both knees on the floor.

You need to change your routine once a month, if not every couple of weeks. Abdominals adapt quickly to exercise, so you have to keep them surprised. You can either change your routine completely or experiment with different variations without changing the order of the exercises or number of repetitions.

For example, in one workout you may want to perform the repetitions quickly to work the fast-twitch muscles and get a good burn. The next time you may do the reps slowly to develop strength and power. Or you can hold each rep in the contracted stage for a second to get a deep muscle contraction. Another method is to do two sets without stopping in between, rest for 20 seconds, and then do another two sets without stopping.

No matter what variation you come up with, always strive for intensity. Never rest longer than 15 to 20 seconds between sets and never stop during a set other than to wait for a muscle cramp to subside—usually five to ten seconds. Always maintain a clear mental image of the abdominal development you want.

Let's take a look at some other abdominal exercises you can use by themselves or as part of a larger routine like the one just described.

Boxer's Twist

This is a two-person exercise that combines an abdominal exercise with a punching movement. It's popular among boxers, and it can be applied easily to a karate punch. Use caution with this one if you have a bad lower back.

Begin on your back as your partner sits on your feet or in some fashion pins them down. Your knees are bent as you raise yourself to about a 45-degree angle, and your fists are held at chin level. Your partner holds his palms out in front of you at shoulder height.

Raise your upper body to a point a little less than vertical (all the way up will take the tension off the abdominals), twist to your right and punch with your left fist at his left palm, and then twist to your left and punch with your right at his right palm. At the completion of the second punch, lower your upper body to the 45-degree angle starting position and then immediately come up again for a second rep and two more punches.

Work yourself up to two sets of 25 reps, pushing yourself to increase your speed with each rep. This exercise will add power to your techniques and help you bob, weave, and duck with speed.

Hook your feet under your partner's legs and lean your upper body back 45 degrees. Sit up quickly and throw a cross punch. Return to the starting position and repeat, cross punching to the other pad.

Leg Throws

This exercise can be quite violent to your lower back, so if you have problems with it or you begin to feel pain from these exercises, stop doing them immediately.

Lie on your back and lift your legs straight up into the vertical position toward your training partner, who is standing behind your head. Your knees are bent slightly and your head and shoulders are raised off the ground a little. Grab your partner's ankles for stability as he takes hold of both of yours and throws them back the way they came up. Your job is to stop the momentum of your legs before they touch the ground and then raise them back up to your partner. He then throws them off to your right side, and again you will stop the momentum and lift them back up.

This is an advanced exercise that works the abdominal area intensely. Make sure your partner throws your legs in all directions so your muscles are attacked from all angles.

Abdominal Machines

Exercise machines that offer some form of resistance to your abdominal work can be used as a way to measure your progress in strength gains. By gradually increasing the number of weight plates, rubber bands, or whatever type of resistance the machine uses, you can easily gauge your progress. If you belong to an athletic club, try out these machines.

Hanging Leg Raises

In bodybuilding circles, hanging leg raises are seldom done because they mostly work the hip flexor muscles at the top of the thigh, muscles of no importance to the aesthetics of bodybuilding. But they are important to you because strong hip flexors add power to your kicks. They are involved in raising the legs past the horizontal plane, a place halfway between horizontal and vertical. This muscle action is found in virtually all kicks delivered waist high and higher.

Here is how you do the exercise. Jump up and grab hold of a high bar. The exercise is performed with bent legs, as

To work your hip flexors and your abs, begin the hanging leg raise by drawing your feet up behind you and raising your knees as high as you can.

opposed to straight legs, because you can lift them higher, thus activating the abdominals once your legs pass horizontal. As you hang, bend your knees about 90 degrees and pull them slightly to your rear to get a good stretch in your hip flexors and abdominals. As you raise your legs as high as you can in front of your body, physically and mentally tense your abs.

Your hip flexors work to raise your legs, as your abdominals flex isometrically to keep your midsection stabilized and provide a base for the flexors. Once your legs are past horizontal, the hip flexors drop out of the action, spinal flexion occurs, and your abdominals contract to rotate your pelvis backward and draw your legs up the rest of the way.

This exercise benefits you in two ways. First, your hip flexors and lower back are strengthened, both of which are involved in lifting your legs in front of your body. Then your abdominals, particularly the lower ones, are worked and strengthened for all the important reasons we discussed earlier.

Hanging leg raises are not easy, especially if your abdominals and your grip are weak. Hand straps will ease your grip on the bar and allow you to fully concentrate on your leg raises. If you can do only three leg lifts, then just do three. But next time go for four. It may take awhile, but make your goal three sets of 10.

Abdominal Toughening

If you don't like getting hit, get out of the martial arts and take up flower arranging. I don't say this to be macho or to insult those people who don't like to be hit in their training. But if you always tell your partner not to hit you or your style pulls their blows three inches from the target, you are training unrealistically. In a real situation, you are going to fall apart psychologically the first time you get struck.

I'm not talking about creating a bloodbath in your training, but I am encouraging you to make light to medium contact regularly and hard contact occasionally in your drills. Let's take a look at an old training technique that is still effective for conditioning you to take medium-power blows to the midsection. Not only does it condition you psychologically, it toughens you physically as well.

Stand in the horse stance between two training partners, who are wearing protective foot gear. The partner on your left throws a roundhouse kick to your midsection, aiming for the area of your belly button. Just as his foot makes contact with your abdomen, mentally and physically tighten your muscles as if you were contracting them outward to meet the blow.

As discussed, you can shout at the point of impact to tighten the abdominal muscles and exhale a burst of air.

Your partner on the right then delivers a roundhouse kick to your middle as you contract your abdominals. Each

Stand in the center as your training partners alternate kicking you in the abdomen.

of your partners should deliver about 10 kicks. Start with light contact and then advance to medium when you are mentally and physically ready. It may take a week, a month, or three months. Eventually, have your training partner put on a pair of foam-rubber safety kicks and throw a set of hard-contact kicks at your middle. Can you deal with it?

Your partners can also hit you with hook kicks, back-fists, and reverse punches. Experiment. Enjoy.

Hitting with a Medicine Ball

In this exercise, a 10-to-20-pound medicine ball is used to strike your midsection. You can do the exercise either standing up or lying down; both have their purposes.

You will feel more impact lying on your back because the hard floor will force you to absorb more of the blow. If you are new to the exercise and have the luxury of a variety of weighted medicine balls, have your partner drop the lightest one first, gradually increasing the weight as your tolerance level goes up.

If you have a heavy medicine ball, your partner should start out dropping it from a low height and gradually increase the distance as your tolerance level improves. Your goal is to have your partner drop the ball from the top of a 30-story building. Just kidding.

When you do the exercise in the standing position, the impact will be less since your back is not braced. Assume your fighting stance and prepare for the blow. Gradually, your partner increases the

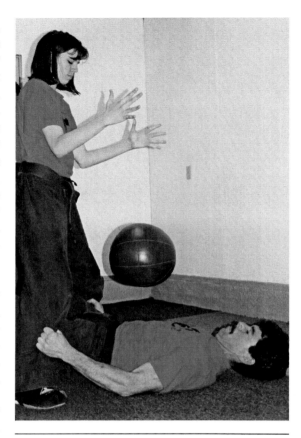

Medicine ball drops condition your abdominals to tolerate punches and kicks.

weight of the ball or, if you have only one, bounce it off you at close range and gradually back up as your tolerance increases.

Always strike the abdominal area, never the relatively fragile rib cage.

Punching the Abs

This is a fun one. You and your partner face each other:

you in the horse stance with your hands on your hips or behind your head and your partner in his fighting stance. His task is to punch you in the middle with both of his gloved hands. How hard you let him hit depends on your condition and tolerance. Work at it until you can take medium to hard impact.

Heavy-Bag Strikes

This exercise requires you to position yourself with a swinging heavy bag so that it strikes you in the abdomen. Stand in a solid stance and push the bag away; then allow it to return and hit you. If you are new to the exercise, don't push the bag too far away. If you are advanced, push it out hard so that it comes back and slams you with greater force.

Here are a couple of impact-conditioning exercises you can do to yourself.

Self-Abuse Exercise 1

Stand in the horse stance with your fisted hands over-head. Bring them down forcefully and strike yourself in the abdomen. You control how hard you hit, your objective being to hit harder and harder. Shout on impact (this is not an exercise to do in an aisle at the supermarket).

Self-Abuse Exercise 2

Combine the first self-abuse exercise with your ab crunches. Lie on your back and place your feet in any position. As you curl into an abdominal crunch, strike your contracted abdominals with the sides or heels of your hands.

• • •

Your entire abdominal-toughening routine shouldn't take more than five minutes. Do about 100 repetitions of any exercise of your choice. You can either do one exercise

Strike yourself repeatedly in the abdominals each time you lift your upper body into a crunch.

for 100 reps or divide up the reps among several exercises that you like. Make it interesting for yourself.

Work your abdominals hard and consistently. A strong and firm midsection is like having supreme gasoline in your tank. It will give you new energy and vitality and add superpower to your punches, kicks, and throws.

CHAPTER ELEVEN

POWERFUL KICKS

Some kickers have incredible power as a result of good genetics and natural strength. But most of the powerful kickers I have known have trained specifically for them.

Here are some exercises and drills that will get you kicking like a pile driver.

HORSE STANCE

The benefits of using the horse as an exercise and as a powerful stance have been discussed several times in this text. Here is another horse exercise that will build pile-driving kicks that the average street fighter will be helpless to stop.

Riding the Plus

My daughter, Amy, who is quite cruel, designed this drill when she was 13 years old. It's one you can practice as is, or use your own creativity to get what you want from it. You can do it holding weights, while executing blocks, or while punching.

She calls it "riding the plus" (+) because you follow a large plus pattern on the floor. Begin by facing forward in a position of attention, hands on your hips. Slide your right foot to the right and drop into a low horse stance. Bring it back to your left foot and resume attention; then slide your left foot to the left into the horse stance. Bring your left foot back to the position of attention and step forward with your left foot as you pivot on your right foot to assume a horse stance facing right. Bring your left foot back to the position of attention, facing forward, and then move your left foot back, pivoting on your right foot until you are in a horse stance facing left. Finish by stepping back to the position of attention facing forward.

This is just one of many ways to ride the plus. You can always step off with the left foot or always step off with the right. You can step backward. You can also cross step, that is, move your right foot to your left and continue until you are in a horse stance facing the opposite direction.

Since the plus pattern consists of lines that are vertical and horizontal, you move only forward and backward and left and right. Now let's take a look at moving diagonally.

Riding the X

Begin this drill as above, standing at attention, facing forward, hands on your hips. Step forward with your left foot at a 45-degree angle from your left and drop into the horse stance. Step back to the position of attention and then step out with your right foot 45 degrees to the right into a horse stance. Bring your right foot back to the position of attention; move your left foot back 45 degrees to your left into a horse stance. Bring your foot back to the position of attention and step back 45 degrees with your right foot into the horse stance. Return to the position of attention.

The X is the basic pattern; how you ride it is up to your imagination. Now let's build on it some more.

Overlapping the Plus and the X

In this drill, which you should do only after you have become smooth in the first two drills, you overlap the plus and X pattern. Draw this on paper and you will see that it forms an asterisk (*), eight directions that address every possible direction you can move offensively and defensively in a fight.

As mentioned before, experiment with different ways of stepping. Use the center as the place you begin and the place you return to each time.

Besides learning to make smooth transitions into a horse stance from different angles, the up-and-down motion of the drill works the leg muscles dramatically. How long you work the drill (that is, how many steps out and back you do) relates to how taxing the drill is to you.

My daughter wanted to make her it harder, so she added the variation illustrated on the following page to totally max-out the legs.

Horse Stance Squats

You can add this to the plus formation, the X formation, or the combined formation. From the upright position of attention, step out in one of the directions and lower yourself into a deep horse stance. Then, without moving your feet, straighten your legs and lower yourself back into a horse stance. In other words, you do a wide-legged squat. Return to the position of attention, move out on whatever line you want, and again perform a squat.

No matter which direction you step or how you step, you always drop into a horse stance, immediately straighten your legs to stand up in place, and lower yourself down into a horse stance again. As you move back to the starting position, raise yourself back up.

To ride the asterisk, begin in its center and step out in any direction you want. Repeat using any of the listed variations.

We are talking about a lot of wide-legged squats here, so it's best to break up the drill. Do 10 reps of stepping and squatting and rest for 30 seconds before you do another 10 reps. If you do too many too soon, you will experience some serious agony the following day. Work up to five to 10 sets.

ANKLE WEIGHTS

You can get one- to three-pound Velcro or strap-on ankle weights in any sporting goods store. Kick at slow-to-medium speed as you proceed through the following drill in one continuous motion, one leg at a time. This isn't a test of balance, so if you start to tilt, just touch the floor with your foot and continue. Save your knees and don't lock out the joint. Here is the sequence:

1. Front kick
2. Roundhouse kick
3. Side kick
4. Back kick

Assume a fighting stance with your left leg forward. Do all four kicks with your right leg and then set it down in front. Now, assume a fighting stance with your right leg forward and do it with your left leg. The number of sets and reps depend on you: your strength and how heavy your ankle weights are. If they aren't heavy, you may want to start out kicking high to fatigue the muscles quickly and then spend the remaining sets kicking at medium and low heights.

SQUAT KICK

Ignore these if you have bad knees. This exercise combines the power-building exercise of the one-legged squat combined with the benefits of repetition kicking. It's a strenuous exercise, one you should build up to slowly.

Begin with a left-leg-forward fighting stance, your arms in an on-guard position. Kneel down with your left knee up and your right knee on the floor, your upper body perfectly straight and balanced. Push yourself into an upright position, using only your left leg, and fire off a front kick with your right. Retract your kick and do a one-legged squat with your left leg as your right returns to the floor.

The stationary leg should do all the work; don't allow your kicking leg to assist your getting up. The entire movement is executed in one smooth action.

This exercise works best with the front kick because of the built-in forward momentum. It can be done the same way with the side kick, but the forward momentum is disrupted when you have to kick sideways. This isn't a big issue; it's just not as smooth as the front kick.

The back kick, however, uses the momentum quite well. Start in the same kneeling position and push yourself

Begin in a kneeling on-guard position and then push off the right leg and launch a left front kick. You can do this exercise slow or fast.

upright with one leg. Execute a back kick, retract your foot to your knee, and drop back to the kneeling position on the floor. Strive for a smooth, uninterrupted flow.

If you have never performed squat kicks before, don't begin with high-repetition sets no matter how good they feel while you are doing them—otherwise you will find out what the term rubber legs means.

Start out with three sets of five reps the first week. Then add one rep to each set per week until you are doing three sets of 10 to 15 per workout.

ONE-LEGGED SQUATS

This is another risky exercise if you have bad knees.

Even if you have good knees, it's wise to go only partway down to minimize stress on the joints.

Assume a neutral stance and extend your right leg forward. Hold your arms out to your sides for balance and slowly lower yourself about one-third of the way and slowly push yourself back up again.

After you have practiced this exercise for awhile, strive to do the repetitions as fast as you can. Your ultimate goal is to pump up and down like a well-oiled machine.

Do three sets of 10 reps with each leg.

One-legged squats will develop powerful thrusting muscles in your legs as long as your knee joints can tolerate them.

RIGID HOPPING

This is good exercise to develop powerful calves, strong feet, and, to a lesser degree, the thrusting muscles of the thighs and hips. It looks a little strange, and it feels even stranger to do, but it's a good power developer.

Stand at attention, feet together, hands along your sides. With as little windup as possible and without using your arms, jump straight up. Then, the instant your feet touch the floor, spring back up again. Repeat for three sets of 10 reps.

LEG SPRINGING

This exercise will develop explosive power in your thighs, particularly valuable for front thrust kicks, side kicks, and any techniques that require you to lower yourself. The concept is simply to jump up on an elevated surface and then jump down again. Stairs work wonderfully because they provide a choice of heights.

Begin in a squatting position, spring up as hard and fast as you can, and land in a squatting position again. Spring back up and drop to the ground where you began.

You can vary the exercise by jumping to different heights, or you can always jump to the same step. The key is to spring explosively on each repetition, land gracefully in a squat, and then spring back to the starting point.

LEG SPRINGING PLYOMETRICALLY

To do the last exercise plyometrically, spring back up the instant your feet hit the floor and the step. There is no pause between jumps, but, rather, an explosive, reflexive spring each time you land. Do three sets of 10 repetitions.

PARTNER JUMPING

This exercise can be a little risky, more for your partner than for you. It not only builds thrusting power in your legs but will get you twisting your hips as well.

Stand beside your partner, who is on his hands and knees, and face toward the direction of his legs. Leap up, tuck your legs underneath you, and twist your body forcefully so that when you land on the other side of him, you will be facing in the same direction as his head. It's a 180-degree turning jump. Do three sets of 10 reps, but if you get tired, stop sooner so that you don't crunch your partner.

PLYOMETRIC HOPPING FOR SPEED

This exercise will develop explosive power and speed in your legs. Begin with your feet about shoulder-width apart, knees bent in preparation to spring. Position your arms

Begin plyometric stair hopping in a squatting position and spring hard up to the third step. Instantly spring back down to the beginning position and spring back up again without pause.

behind you so that they can snap forward to assist in your leap. Jump and pull your feet up to your buttocks at the apex and then bring them down to land. To make the exercise plyometric, constantly strive to minimize your contact with the floor. Leap up, come down, touch the floor, and then reflexively explode up again. Don't allow your arms to flail or go in a circle. Swoop them up and then bring them straight down as you drop to the floor.

Think speed and you will develop speed. Do three sets of 15 reps.

PLYOMETRIC HOPPING FOR POWER

This variation is similar to the last exercise, except that this one is primarily to develop explosive power.

Begin as in the last exercise and jump up as high as you can, pulling your knees up high and drawing your feet to your buttocks. The instant you touch the ground, spring back again. Don't hesitate and don't take a deep breath or the time to gather your strength. To be plyometric, you must spring back without pausing.

You may want to modify the intensity; this exercise can be quite vigorous, especially if you are new to it. For example, when doing a 10-rep set, cut back on the intensity by jumping high only on the even numbers and half as high on the odd numbers. You still need to spring right back up each time your feet touch to make the exercise plyometric.

PLYOMETRIC HOPPING FOR DISTANCE

This is more intense than the above two hopping exercises and a little riskier because you are striving for distance. You need to be cautious about how you land; any kind of distraction could cause you to land awkwardly and be injured.

Start out as in the first two exercises but, instead of going straight up, leap out as far as you can. Continuously

strive to cover greater distance, using your arms to help with your thrust. The instant your feet touch the ground, spring back up and forward as forcefully as you can. Land flat-footed to prevent injury to your toes, ankles, and the balls of your feet.

CHAIR KICKS

Begin in an on-guard position with one foot on a chair (left) and then drive yourself up into a standing position and launch a front kick.

This is one of those exercises you love to hate. You love it because you will see a rapid increase in your leg power, and you hate it because it will wipe out your energy reserves and leave you with wobbly legs. The only equipment you need is a steady, hard-bottomed chair.

Begin by standing in front of the chair in a left-leg-forward fighting stance, with your left leg on the seat of the chair. Using the strength of your front leg (not momentum), bring your right leg into a high, chambered position, and execute a high front thrust kick. Return your leg to the chambered position and lower yourself to the floor.

If this isn't bad enough, there are a couple of ways you

can add to the intensity. When lifting your rear leg up into the high chambered position, strive to straighten your front leg as slowly as possible, as if you were doing the top half of a very slow squat. The slower you come up, the greater the intensity. After you have kicked, return your foot to the chambered position and slowly lower it to the floor.

Another variation is to kick slowly. Once you have risen from the floor and chambered the kick, s-l-o-w-l-y extend your foot out to full extension. It won't be as high as when you kicked fast, but that's OK. Just go as high as you are able and hold it there for two seconds. Be honest with the time: count to yourself, "One-thousand-one, one-thousand-two," and then retract it and lower your foot back to the floor.

If you do the repetitions at regular speed, work up to three sets of eight reps. If you are doing any of the slow variations, increase your rest period between sets and work up to three sets of five reps.

Since you liked slow kicking so much, here are some more. If you are not disciplined, you will come up with a zillion reasons why you shouldn't do these. But if you are mentally tough, and do them on a regular basis, you will develop powerful legs.

SLOW FRONT KICKS

Take hold of something for support so that you can kick as high as possible. Begin with your foot on the floor and slowly raise it to your highest chambered position. This strengthens the exact muscles of the hip and upper thigh that lift your knee into the chambered position. Some fighters isolate the knee-lift exercise from the kick so that they can concentrate on the chambering muscles. This can be especially beneficial if you feel that your chambering is slow or you want to develop power in your front knee strike. Do three sets of 10.

Now for the extension. Hold on to something for support so that you can concentrate on the muscles being worked rather than on your balance, and so that you can kick high-er, thus adding even more intensity to the exercise.

S-l-o-w-l-y extend your flexed foot. When you have reached full extension, hold the position for two or three seconds to ensure that all the muscles are contracted. Bring your foot back at whatever speed you want and slowly kick out again.

The slower and higher the kick, the more miserable—er, the more *beneficial*—the exercise. If you do the kicks simul-taneously with a partner, the person who extends his foot more slowly is the winner. Sweat out two sets of 10 reps.

SLOW ROUNDHOUSE KICKS

The muscles exercised with slow front kicking are near-ly the same ones used in the extension portion of the slow roundhouse kick. For that reason, you may want to put most of your effort into working the muscles involved in chambering the roundhouse.

Hold on to a support and slowly lift your chambered leg as high as you can. Upon reaching your highest point, lean over a little more on the support and force your muscles to lift your leg a tad bit higher. Don't jerk your leg up the addi-tional distance; move slowly and smoothly and make your muscles work for it.

Once you have completed your chambering sets, do two sets of 10 reps of just the extension. Simply extend your leg slowly, hold it for two or three seconds, and retract it. Angle the kick up a little to get some gravity resistance. Do two sets of 10 reps.

SLOW SIDE KICKS

There are several ways you can practice slow kicking with the side kick. All of them are good, and they each attack the muscles a little differently.

Variation 1

Assume a horse stance. This isn't an exercise for the horse stance, so you can sit as high or as low as you like. Lift your right knee into the chambered position and slowly extend your foot until your knee locks out. Hold for a count of two; then retract your foot and set it back on the floor. Do three sets of 10 reps with both legs.

Variation 2

In this variation, perform the sidekick slowly as in the first exercise, but kick just above your training partner's open palm. Hold your foot there for a moment and then lift it a couple of inches above his palm. Hold it for a count of two and then retract your foot back to the floor. Know that you may experience an intense cramp in your hip muscles.

Variation 3

Get on your hands and knees and tuck your left arm underneath you so that your shoulder is resting on the floor. From this awkward position, slowly kick straight up with your right leg. This will force you to fight gravity as you push your side kick straight to the sky. Do three sets of 10 reps.

Variation 4

Stand with your shoulder next to a wall, your closest foot about 12 inches away from it. Hold your outside leg stiff and slowly raise it to the side as high as you can (which won't be too high). Hold for a two-second count and then lower it to the floor. Do three sets of 10 reps.

SLOW BACK KICK

Slow back kicks will strengthen your back kicks as well as firm your back porch. The glutes are perhaps the strongest muscles of the body and, when conditioned, will give you a kick as strong as Superman's.

Variation 1

Assume your fighting stance and lift your rear foot off the floor to the knee of your stationary leg. Slowly kick straight back as high as you can until your leg is straight. Hold for a two-second count; retract your foot and place it back on the floor. Do three sets of 10 reps with each leg.

Variation 2

Get down on all fours and slowly kick back and up with your right leg. Hold the extended position for a two-second count before you retract your foot back to the floor. Do three sets of 10 reps.

You can expect muscle cramping when kicking slowly, more with some kicks than with others. Although this will pass with time and improved strength, you can usually make it disappear by shaking it out or with massage. If it returns, try kicking lower so there is less stress on the muscles. If that doesn't help, stop the exercise and try it again the next day.

STICKY FOOT

This is another painful exercise that will knot up the thigh and hip muscles to let you know, in no uncertain terms, which ones are involved in the kick. Although the objective is to develop power in the exact muscles you want to be strong, you will also develop greater control over your kicks so that you can easily put your foot exactly where you want it.

The drill here is to kick out to full extension (just short of total joint lockout) and hold the extension for two or three seconds. You can practice this with the four basic kicks (front, roundhouse, back, and side), using the front leg or the rear leg. You can do it in the air by yourself, against a wall or post, or with a partner.

Face your partner in your fighting stance and launch a front kick at his midsection. When your foot makes controlled contact, hold it there for two seconds as if it was stuck and then snap it back to your support leg and return it to the floor. You do 10 in a row; then your partner does 10. Or you can each do one at a time, trading back and forth until you have reached the desired number of reps.

Work both legs and do all four kicks. Do them fast or do them slow, but whichever speed you choose, your objective is to hold each kick for two or three seconds at the extension.

You may want to do them from time to time with ankle weights to add even greater resistance. I highly recommend that you do the repetitions slowly to preserve the life of your joints.

As your strength improves in this exercise, kick higher and higher to make the muscles work harder and harder. If your leg muscles knot up, simply lower your leg and shake out the knot and the accompanying pain and then continue with the exercise.

OK, that's enough slow kicking. Let's take a look at a tri-set, three exercises performed one after the other. These are intense enough that you don't need to do any other leg exercises other than what you normally do during your martial arts training. Do these twice a week on nonclass days.

DUMBBELL TRI-SET LUNGES

I occasionally like to combine weight resistance exercises with karate repetitions. You must be cautious about using too much weight, though, because it can tighten your muscles and make your karate movements stiff, even painful, especially if you practice your fighting art right after you lift. As always, experiment to see what works best for you.

The following tri-set will give you powerful kicks, if you can survive the routine. You rest only after the third set, but for just 60 seconds, and then the three exercises are repeated. You may use a barbell, but I like to use dumbbells because they are easier to handle and more fun. Grab a couple of light ones, say 10-pounders, just until you get the feel for the first movement, the lunges. The movement may be a little awkward at first and may take a few repetitions to establish a groove.

To begin, stand straight and hold the dumbbells down at your sides. Maintain a straight posture throughout the entire exercise. Step straight out with your left foot about as far as you would step when executing a deep forward stance. At full extension, your rear leg should be bent so that the knee lightly touches the floor. Pause for a second, then drive off the forward foot, and step back to the starting position. Do it with your right foot on the next rep and then continue back and forth until you have completed 10 reps with each leg. Lunges work all parts of the upper leg, especially the muscles around the knees.

Without stopping to rest, move on to the dead lifts. This is a great exercise for the back of the legs. If you have never done dead lifts before, don't underestimate them. It may not feel like you are getting at the hamstrings, but if you do too many at first or go too heavy, you will curse yourself.

Start the exercise from the same position as in the lunges. Your feet are about shoulder-width apart, dumbbells held at arm length in front of your thighs. Keep your legs straight and bend forward at your waist until the dumbbells touch the floor. When you straighten back to the upright position, use your hamstrings and glutes to lift the weights, not your lower back. Do 10 reps per set.

Strive for smooth execution in both the lunges and the dead lifts. Stay balanced, keep your body in alignment, and perform the repetitions at a pace much slower than you would execute a martial art technique, but faster than you would normally perform a weight-lifting exercise.

The third phase of this routine is to kick. I usually do front, back, and roundhouse kicks because they use different muscles. Depending on your experience and condition, you want to do each kick with each leg between 25 and 50 times.

This tri-set is a real power developer. Begin in the ready position and lunge out and return 10 times with each leg. Immediately do 10 reps of stiff-legged dead lifts. Bend over until the dumbbells nearly touch the floor and then stand back up. Go immediately into a set of 25 to 50 kicks.

This is how you set up your routine. Do a set of lunges, followed by a set of dead lifts, followed by a set of front kicks. Rest a minute and then do the lunges and dead lifts again, this time followed by a set of roundhouse kicks. Then do a final set of lunges and dead lifts, completing the tri-set with a set of back kicks. You rest only after the third exercise, not between individual exercises.

You will definitely feel this, and you will reap the benefits in just a few weeks.

SHIN TOUGHENING

If your training partner thinks it hurts when you kick him in the ribs with the top of your foot, next time kick him with your shinbone and listen to him power snivel. Without a doubt, the shin is an excellent weapon, especially against soft targets like the neck, floating ribs, kidneys, and inner and outer thighs. It's also effective against hard targets, such as the head, elbow joint, kneecap, and your opponent's shin—but the impact can be equally devastating to your own leg if your shin hasn't been conditioned.

Can you toughen this weapon to deliver powerful kicks to hard surfaces without causing acute pain to yourself? Yes, you can. Is the process painful? Yup.

Here is a three-stage shin-toughening plan that has been used successfully by many full-contact fighters. It's best to start out easy, and expect it to take about six months of progressive training to get your shins to a point where you can kick hard surfaces without a lot of pain to your own leg.

Stage 1

Obtain a heavy cardboard cylinder, the type found inside large rolls of industrial-sized paper. Sit on the floor and simply roll the cylinder up and down your shins for 15 to 20 minutes, pressing the cardboard harder and harder as your pain tolerance increases over the days.

Stage 2

After your shin has become conditioned to Stage 1, wrap an unopened pop bottle with two layers of cloth and then roll it up and down your shin. When that no longer causes discomfort, remove the cloth and just use the bare bottle. Some fighters use an old wooden rolling pin, first wrapping it in cloth and then removing it after the shin has toughened.

Stage 3

The final step, which could take from three to six months, is to gently tap the shins with the pop bottle or the rolling pin, pushing yourself to strike progressively harder and harder as the weeks roll by. Some fighters advance to a point where they routinely tap their shins with a hammer or a barbell plate.

In time, your shins will be conditioned to withstand tremendous impact. You will be able to whip a powerful shin kick through your opponent's shin or forearm block and send him to the floor writhing in pain.

POWER STRETCHING

I know a guy who is a living Gumby: he can do the splits, put his heel behind his head, and bend all the way over backwards. But he can't kick high. In fact, he can barely kick to his opponent's waist. He has the flexibility, but he has no strength in it. Although this is common in people with natural flexibility, it's also seen in people who have trained to improve their stretch but have done nothing to put power in it.

Power in a flexible muscle doesn't happen on its own; you have to train for it specifically. It's an effort, but the results will amaze you. Here are a few exercises that develop flexibility and power.

The student on the right pushes his partner's legs out to her maximum stretch for 20 to 30 seconds. Then she presses inward against his feet for six seconds as he slowly allows her legs to move in a few inches.

Sitting Stretch

To work the inner thigh and groin muscles, sit on the floor and spread your legs as far as possible. Your partner should sit across from you and place his feet inside your ankles so that he can push your legs out to your maximum stretch.

Hold this position for 20 to 30 seconds. To develop power in the stretched muscle, push in against his feet for 10 seconds. Your partner lets you succeed by slowly moving his feet in, but only 12 inches with each foot. He should make this a smooth movement for you, but one that makes you work hard for every inch.

When you go to do a second set of these, you will be happily surprised to find your maximum stretch has increased a couple of inches. Repeat for five or six sets, resting about 30 seconds in between.

Wishbone Stretch

This two-person stretch works the hamstrings—the muscles on the back of the legs—and to a lesser degree the muscles on the front of the thigh. This a favorite among fighters who like to use the ax kick.

With your back to a wall, have your partner lift your right leg as high as it can go. Depending on you and your partner's height difference, he may be able to support your foot on his shoulder or he may have to use his hands to push your leg up to its maximum range. Hold for 20 to 30 seconds and then press your foot down against your partner's hands or shoulder. He should offer moderate resistance, allowing you to lower your foot 12 to 15 inches, taking about 10 seconds to do so. At the conclusion of each repetition, you will probably be able to stretch higher than on the last one. Do five reps with each leg.

Roundhouse Kick Stretch

Lean against a wall and chamber your leg as if preparing to throw a roundhouse kick, leaning away as far as you normally do when kicking. Your partner grasps your ankle and knee and pushes your leg up into your maximum stretch, holding it in place for 20 to 30 seconds. At the completion of the stretch, slowly extend your foot in the kick as your partner provides resistance against your ankle. He should resist through the full extension, which should last about 10 seconds. Work both legs for five reps each.

To put power in the chambered position of the kick, chamber your leg as high as you can and have your partner push it even higher for 20 to 30 seconds. Then have him provide resistance as you lower it. Do five reps with each leg.

Hook Kick Stretch

Lean against a wall just as you did with the roundhouse kick. Chamber your leg, then extend it to where you start the hook phase of the kick. Your partner then takes hold of your foot and pushes your leg up to its maximum stretch

To build power in your groin muscles, press your knees down with your hands or elbows for 20 to 30 seconds. Then press your knees up against hard resistance for six seconds.

for 20 to 30 seconds. This also stretches the inside thigh and groin muscles that aid the side kick. At the completion of the stretch, begin to hook your leg as your partner offers resistance through the track.

Do five reps with each leg. The kick phase should take no more than 10 seconds.

Butterfly Stretch

I like to do this one with my back against something, though many people do it without the support. It works the inner thigh muscles that are so important in the side and crescent kick.

Sit on the floor and draw your feet to your groin area so that the heels are touching. Use your hands to push your knees down as far as they can go without discomfort, and hold for 20 to 30 seconds. Then use your hands to offer resistance as you slowly raise your knees. Allow your knees to win but not without a struggle. Do two sets of 10 reps.

It's important that your partner gives steady resistance throughout the full range of the movements. Uneven, jerky resistance is not only ineffective, but potentially dangerous. Do the exercises as if you were doing them on a smooth exercise machine.

CHAPTER TWELVE

POWER PUNCHING AND STRIKING

There are several types of straight-line punches: reverse, jab, straight, inverted, and other variations indigenous to specific martial art systems. Of the circular variety, there are roundhouse punches, uppercuts, hooks, claws, and a number of others. It doesn't matter how you configure your hand when striking in a straight or circular direction of force because that has little to do with the power of the blow. Hand configuration determines the type of injury: scrape, deep penetration, blunt trauma, etc.

To hit hard, you must bring into play certain body mechanics and other factors that have been mentioned over and over throughout this text: relaxed muscles, hip rotation, forward momentum, driving leg thrust, mental intent, and physical strength. Each element plays an important part in the chain of power. Eliminate one and you weaken the chain. Would you have confidence in a chain with a weak or broken link?

I am not going to insult you, your instructor, or your system and tell you there is a better way to punch than the way you do. If you are executing your punch the way your teacher taught you, it has remained in your fighting system because it has stood the test of time. But all of us must evaluate our technique from time to time to see that all the power elements are there and that we are getting the most out of them. Occasional review never hurts.

Let's take a look at the following important elements to ensure that you are punching with maximum power.

THE ROLE OF YOUR LEGS

- Use a stance that allows you to rotate your waist with the blow.
- Stay light on your feet so that you can move in and out of range with speed.
- Consider moving on the balls of your feet to create a sense of lightness and to enable you to move fast in all directions.
- When throwing a rear-hand punch, come off your rear heel and drive with the ball of your foot. This increases your power and gives you greater extension into the target.
- To get even more extension, slightly bend your front knee an instant before your punch hits the target.
- When you shuffle or lunge in to punch, plant your lead foot as your fist lands. This creates a strong stance and adds to the impact of your blow.

THE ROLE OF YOUR ABDOMINALS

- When your punch is about an inch away from the target, contract your stomach muscles as hard as you can. Much power comes from your center.

THE ROLE OF YOUR HIPS

* A whiplike snap of your waist can increase the impact of a punch nearly twofold.

THE ROLE OF YOUR MIND

* If you believe you are going to hit with power, you will.
* If you think you are weak, your punch will be weak.
* Visualize hitting through the target.

BENCH PRESS

There is much more involved in a punch than just your fist striking a target. For example, the straight punch depends on the shoulder muscles to initiate movement; the shoulder, triceps, and pec muscles to drive the fist outward; the forearm muscles to rotate the fist; and the shoulder, biceps, and forearm muscles to prevent overextension of the arm and to retract the fist. Here's the good news: all of these muscles are involved in the bench-press exercise.

I think the bench press is one of the best power developers for straight-line punching there is. When performed correctly—and correctly is the key word here—it will give you tremendous punching power.

There are so many variations of the bench press that it would take an entire book to address them all. Whether you use a bar or dumbbells is a matter of preference. It's not a bad idea to switch from one to the other every couple of months to give your muscles variety and a little shock. You get a better stretch with dumbbells because you can lower them farther, but some lifters find them too awkward to handle. Other lifters favor the solid feel of a barbell. Again, it's up to you.

It's not important to be able to bench phenomenal weights to be able to hit hard. Your goal it to develop power that can translate into your punching. By training consistently and pushing yourself gradually to increase the weight, you will improve quickly. Save the power lifting for the power lifters.

You can do most of the following exercises on a bench-press machine. Keep in mind that machines balance the weight for you, making it easier to get into the groove of the exercise. Although this sounds good, it actually reduces the number of muscles involved in the press. The end result is that your strength gains will be less than when using free weights.

Standard Bench Presses

The standard bench press is invaluable for those fighters who are just starting to supplement their training with weights or for those who don't want to get fancy but want to add some applicable resistance to get more power in their punches. You can use dumbbells or a barbell.

Space your hands on the bar a little outside the width of your shoulders, or if you are using dumbbells, hold them a little beyond the same width. (I have known a lot of people over the years who have ruined their shoulder joints by bench pressing too widely. They did so under the misconception that using a wide grip would develop a wide chest. Sorry, but only God can change your physical structure. Using a wide grip on the bench will not widen your chest, but it will put stress on your shoulders and underlying skeletal system. A shoulder-width grip will not only save your shoulders, but will put your hands and arms in the precise position in which you straight-line punch.)

Do one light-weight set of 15 reps. On the next two or three sets, increase the weight so that you have to push moderately hard on your tenth repetition. Do three sets of 10 reps.

Exploding Bench Presses

This is an excellent exercise to develop explosive power, though it's not quite as ominous as it sounds. The set and rep count is entirely up to you, your physical condition, and your experience with weights.

Lie on your back under a weight that you can do eight reps with and lower it to your chest at a pace you normally use. To explode, push the bar forcefully upward as you exhale, stopping just short of lockout to prevent stress on your elbow joints. Lower the bar to your chest and again push it forcefully upward. The explosive movement approximates the explosive thrust of your punch. You are activating the fast-twitch muscles and conditioning them to accelerate with force. As always, don't lock out your elbows at the end of the movement.

Dumbbell Rotation Presses

The value of this exercise is that using dumbbells allows you to rotate your hands as you do when punching. Lie on your back and hold the weights at your chest, rotating your hands so that your palms are facing toward your head. If the dumbbells are too heavy, begin the movement with your palms facing inward toward your body. Since rotating your hands prevents you from using your usual weight, use this exercise in conjunction with another benching movement.

As you press the dumbbells upward, rotate your hands as if you were punching. I am always cautious of doing this move too fast since the twisting motion is somewhat stressful to the muscles surrounding the elbow. Use too much speed and weight and you just might get a major tweak somewhere in your arms.

Close-Grip Bench Press

Bodybuilders like this exercise because it adds size to the triceps on the back of the arm. Power lifters use it as a power-developing exercise to supplement their bench press work. It's a good exercise for power development since its track follows the punch very closely.

Grip the bar in the middle, your hands about a fist-

To add resistance to the reverse punch, hold two dumbbells at chest level with your palms facing in. Rotate your hands slowly as if punching until your arms are extended.

width apart. If you haven't done this exercise before, use a light weight until you develop a feel for the groove. Some lifters lower the bar to their nipples, others lower it to their

Close-grip bench presses will help you develop tremendous punching power. Grip the bar about a fist-width apart and raise and lower the weight.

nose, and still others lower it somewhere in between. You will have to experiment.

If you want to work all three heads of your triceps and duplicate the motion of your straight-line punches, hold your elbows in close to your sides. If you want to work the outer heads for a little variety, wing your elbows out.

Slow and Heavy, Light and Fast

This is a simple variation I use from time to time. It can be done with any method of benching you choose and is based on a twice-a-week schedule. In one workout you do the exercise heavy and slow; in the next you do it light and fast. The order doesn't matter, just go by how you feel.

The heavy day is your power workout. Choose a weight you can use for about six reps; the last two reps should be a hard push. You may even want to consider a training partner to "spot" the weight so that you can use heavy poundage without fear. Do a warm-up set with a light weight and then do three heavy sets, with a minute's rest in between.

There are all kinds of variations on how to stagger your weight and reps when going heavy. For example, choose a weight for the first set that you can barely lift for about eight reps. Increase the weight so that you can barely squeeze out six reps on the second heavy set and then reduce the weight a little to squeeze out another six reps on the third set.

On the light day, reduce your poundage so that you can pump out eight to twelve reps faster than you normally do. The last one or two reps should be done at a moderate level of intensity, but not at the artery-bursting level you do on your heavy day. Do a warm-up set followed by three sets of light and fast reps.

The idea here is to build power on the heavy days and to work for speed and muscle endurance on light days.

Dead Stops

This is a difficult exercise so you don't need to do it every workout. In fact, most weight lifters use it every third workout in order to allow the muscles time to recuperate. It's a good exercise for developing power and speed at the take-off stage of a straight-line punch.

Choose any method of bench pressing you want. Lower the bar to your chest as you normally do but pause for one to two seconds and then push the weight back to the starting position. One or two sets of six reps should do it.

PLYOMETRIC MEDICINE BALL CATCH

This is a simple exercise of playing catch with a medicine ball. The balls come in varying weights, so get one that is heavy enough to tax your muscles yet light enough to allow you to do the exercise with good form. This works the triceps, shoulders, chest, and back muscles, the very muscles involved in punching.

You and your partner stand apart but close enough so that the thrown ball doesn't arc. When your partner thrusts the ball to you, allow its weight to force your arms back toward your chest and then reflexively and forcefully thrust the ball back. To ensure that the exercise is plyometric, don't pause; thrust it away from you as if it were a huge, burning coal.

A variation is to lie on your back and have your partner drop the ball toward your chest. Your job is to catch the ball and thrust it back up as quickly as you can.

WEIGHTED PUNCHES

I like these because I have made tremendous gains from them. My daughter has been doing them for six months and has virtually doubled her power on the heavy bag. Weighted punches are directly applicable to the punching motion because punching is exactly what you are doing in the exercise.

You can do these when you practice your fighting art or supplemental training. Because they work the front deltoid muscles, I incorporate them into my shoulder routine when I lift weights.

To make this exercise plyometric, catch the medicine ball close to your body and allow the weight to sink close to your chest before you immediately thrust it back up to your partner.

Cable Punching

I included this in *Speed Training* as an exercise to develop speed. It will do that, but it will also develop power when you progressively increase the weight.

Cables that angle downward from a point at head height or higher are sometimes awkward to work with, and I'm not convinced that the angle stimulates the punching muscles where they should be stimulated, anyway. The ideal setup is to have the cable extend out from the floor or from a point about even with your belt or chest.

Start with your back to the cable device and use a palm-up grip on the handle, holding it at your hip or a little higher if that is your style. Even if you don't normally start your punch from this traditional place, doing so in this exercise will give you a greater range of movement. Extend the handle straight out from the center of your body and roll your hand over as if you were punching.

Three sets of 10 reps with both arms are enough. Work to slowly increase the weight, but not so much that your form suffers. Remember, you are just *exercising* your punching muscles, you are not out to set a world record. Advance slowly, maintain good form, and watch your power increase.

Dumbbell Punching

This is basically the same exercise as with the cables except that you have more freedom to punch in different directions. You can use one dumbbell at a time or hold one in each hand and alternate your punches.

Choose a weight that gives you comfortable resistance for 12 to 15 repetitions. Think of this as a "heavy hands" exercise. The idea is not to push superheavy weight and use forced reps as you do when you are trying to reach new poundage in your bench press. Your objective is to simply add resistance to your punching muscles and slowly increase the weight when it feels right. If you take a conservative approach, you will maintain good form and stay on track with the movement.

Although there are a number of ways you can punch, it's

You can practice punches with wrist weights or dumbbells.

important to do the same movement for three sets. If you do a different punch every set or, worse, every rep, the muscles involved in one specific punch will not be worked sufficiently.

If you want to sit in the horse stance and alternately punch straight out, do it that way consistently for three sets. If you want to work two different punches, do two sets of each, such as two sets for reverse punches and two sets for uppercuts. Or you may want to do three sets of one type of punch for a month and three sets of another the next month.

Here is how I do mine using two dumbbells. I stand in a high fighting stance, my hands held where I normally hold them when punching. I then launch a reverse punch, being careful not to fully extend and lock the elbow joint. As it retracts, I launch a lead-arm straight punch. I rotate my hips on each punch and consciously extend my energy outward with each blow. Sometimes I punch slowly; other times I increase the speed, although I never go fast. I fluctuate the height of my reps, going from a 45-degree angle upward to a 45-degree angle downward. I do more of the upper-angle punches because gravity places more stress on the muscles. I do 12 to 15 reps and then switch stances and do another set. I do the straight-line punches with wrist rotation for a month and then switch to inverted punches (these are straight punches with the palms facing up throughout the entire movement). Though the direction of force and the motion of the inverted punch are still straight, the inverted fist position places a different stress on the shoulders and chest.

Wrist Weights

These exercises could also be included in Chapter 3, "Ancient Exercises," because they were practiced many years ago. However, resistance devices are different today, and our knowledge of the body and scientific training concepts has dramatically improved over the past couple of hundred years.

Today you can Velcro on some wrist weights rather than hold on to a big river rock, or strapon ankle weights rather than place iron rings around your ankles, as was done many years ago. Although weight is weight, modern-day wrist and ankle weights are easier and safer to use, and can be bought cheaply wherever athletic equipment is sold.

As mentioned many times in this text, it's important when adding weight to your punches and kicks not to lock out your joints. This is never a good idea without weights, and it's a terrible idea with them. I am convinced that I have lasted in the martial arts since 1965 because I have always used caution with my joints. I taught myself early on not to extend all the way out with my punches and kicks, and I have never trained fast with supplemental weight.

It should be noted, however, that some people do train fast while wearing or holding weights, and they claim they do so without problems. Maybe. It could be that problems just haven't manifested themselves yet but will in a few years. Or it may be that the fighter is blessed with joints that will never be affected. Personally, I don't think it's worth the risk.

The following arm drills will strengthen the very muscles you want to be powerful. You can do them fast if you like, but, again, I strongly advise you to do high repetitions at medium speed without snapping the joint. Do them in one continuous motion so that you not only work the specific muscles of the technique, but the transition muscles as well. Use any stance you want, although a deep or shallow horse stance provides equal treatment for each arm. Flow through the sequence in this order.

1. Left straight punch
2. Right straight punch
3. Left high backfist
4. Right high backfist
5. Left rising block
6. Right rising block
7. Left lower block
8. Right lower block
9. Left outside block
10. Right outside block
11. Left inside block
12. Right inside block

Use good form and repeat until fatigued.

POWERFUL FOREARMS

A student once told me that he would like to develop a grip so powerful that he could reach out and grab an assailant by the face and squeeze until the guy had to plead for mercy. Well, I don't know how sound that is tactically, but if he were to follow the forearm routine listed here he would easily achieve his goal. Powerful forearms will dramatically add to your striking, punching, grappling, and weapons skills. And, visually, muscular forearms can be intimidating to some would-be attackers.

There are lots of myths floating around about forearms. Perhaps the biggest one is that they are tough, sinewy muscles used so much in our daily activities that they will respond only to high-repetition exercise.

Before I address that, consider this word of caution about the many myths surrounding bodybuilding (and there are many): abdominals require hundreds of reps; African Americans can't develop their calves; wide-grip bench presses build a wide chest; large quantities of protein build big muscles; a muscular physique attracts the opposite sex.

Never accept such absolutes at face value. They may be true, they may have a bit of truth in them, or they may be total nonsense.

Forearms do require hard work, but no more than any other muscle group (contrary to what Bruce Lee believed). Training must be consistent and must involve all the muscles of the forearms, in particular the three major muscle groups: flexors, extensors, and the brachioradialis. Flexors run along the bottom of the forearms and are used to bend and flex the wrist. The extensors are located along the top of the forearms and are involved in extending and straightening the wrist. The brachioradialis, located on top of your forearm near the elbow, works with your biceps to bend your elbow joint. Never work just one muscle without working the others. If you work the flexors without working the extensors, you will actually be building a weakness in your development that may lead to injury.

You only need to do six to ten repetitions when working the forearms, though the common belief is that you need to do more. Studies show that high-rep sets for forearms gets the same results as do six to ten reps. So why do more? Keep the sets at about three to four per exercise with a maximum of about 15 sets for your entire forearm routine. All reps should take no more than two seconds to complete.

Although the following forearm exercises have been around for a long time, I'm going to throw in some variations that will increase their effectiveness.

Wrist Curls

Grab a barbell loaded with enough weight to do six to ten reps, straddle a bench, and place your forearms over its edge. Normally, lifters are taught not to extend their arms

Extend your forearms about one-third of their length and lower the weights until your elbows are off your legs. As your wrists curl the weights upward, allow your elbows to lower onto your thighs.

past the wrists, but in this variation half your arm will extend over the edge. Position your thighs so that they support the sides of your forearms.

As you lower the weight, allow your elbows to come off the bench until your forearms are at a downward 45-degree angle. Then as you curl the weight up, lower your elbows back to the bench. This maneuver will force continuous resistance on your forearm flexor muscles, more than other variations.

Reverse Wrist Curls

To work the extensors, curl the barbell with your palms facing down as usual, but add the following variation to make the exercise even more effective.

Sit on a bench and place your forearms on your thighs so that your elbows are angled toward the outside of your legs and your wrists are extended over the inside of your knees. Position your legs so that your hands are at shoulder width or a little more than shoulder width apart.

As you lower the weight, allow your elbows to come up off your thighs so that your forearms are at a 45-degree angle. As you curl the weight up, lower your elbows and move them inward so that by the time the weight has reached its maximum height, your forearms are parallel with each other. As you do this, simultaneously come up on your toes. Then as you lower the weight, lower your heels and let your forearms move outward at an angle and once again raise them off your thighs.

This is not as complicated as it sounds, though it does take a little conscious coordination at first. You might want to do a few dry runs without weight to establish the movement. It's well worth the effort to learn because it places a greater workload on the extensor muscles than other variations.

Behind-the-Back Wrist Curl

It's important to do two flexor exercises in your routine since it has been found that two effect greater forearm growth.

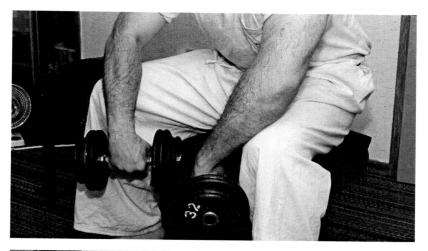

Angle your forearms in and down inside your legs. As you rotate your hands up, move your elbows in so your forearms are horizontal and in line with your thighs.

I have a love-hate relationship with this exercise. I love the muscle pump I get from it, but I hate the pain. This can be done with the bench press attachment on a Nautilus machine or with a free weight. When using the machine, set the pin to the weight you want, back up to the machine, grasp the handles, and perform the curls. When using a barbell, lay the weight on a bench and back up to it. In both cases, assume a grip a little narrower than shoulder width and let the bar roll down to the ends of your fingers. Curl the weight up, hold the contracted position for a second, and then lower it back to the ends of your fingers.

For variety, try the exercise with dumbbells.

Reverse Curls

This is a long-time favorite that directly attacks the brachioradialis muscle on top of the forearm near the elbow. Grasp a barbell with a shoulder-width grip, palms down, and curl the bar up until your forearms are a little higher than parallel with the floor. Don't let your elbows flare out, but, rather, keep them along your sides. You must concentrate on your brachioradialis, or your biceps will take on too much of the load.

I like to do what I call a double reverse curl to hit the wrists as well as the big forearm muscles. I begin the exercise as mentioned but flex my palms to curl the bar back toward my legs as far as I can go. Then, as I curl my forearms upward, I also curl my wrists upward. By the time my forearms are a little higher than horizontal with the floor, which is as far as I go, my wrists have curled the weight back to full contraction. This hurts a little, but deeply stimulates the muscles.

Work your forearms at the end of your weight routine so that your arms won't be too tired to work your other body parts. This allows you to use heavy weights without having to conserve energy for other exercises.

ONE-INCH PUNCH

The one-inch punch was made popular by Bruce Lee during a demonstration at Ed Parker's International Karate

Begin the forearm curl by flexing your hands inward. Raise the bar until your forearms are above horizontal and flex your hands up as far as you can.

Championships in 1964. With a nearly imperceptible movement, he knocked a much larger man back several feet and left the crowd with its collective mouth hanging open.

Although the effects of the punch do look supernatural, those martial artists who have mastered it know that it's actually a synchronization of many body parts. As the name implies, the punch is delivered no more than one inch from the target without retracting the fist. Since most people associate a punch with a fist that is first cocked and then launched across a space of at least 12 inches before it makes contact, the one-inch punch does indeed look like something from another world.

The punch has some applicability to self-defense since it's quite capable of causing internal damage. But perhaps its real value is that through the process of learning and practicing it, you will enhance your ability to combine all your muscles into one explosive move.

Basics of the One-Inch Punch

As mentioned, the power of the punch comes from the perfectly timed synchronization of the arms, legs, feet, shoulders, and hips into one explosive microsecond. But to the untrained eye, it looks like one lightning-quick movement.

Get a large coffee can, fill it with sand, and tape the lid shut. You may want to consider wrapping a piece of carpet or some other type of padding around it if you have sensitive hands or skin. Set the can on the edge of a table or some other smooth surface so that it will slide away when you punch it.

Stand before the table and assume a comfortable stance that works for you. It doesn't matter which stance your training partner uses because his may not work for your body structure.

You may find you can execute the technique with little footwork, or you may need to incorporate a thrust. To use footwork, position yourself in front of the can with your stronger side forward. Some people start the move with the heel of their lead foot raised; others simply pivot on the ball of their foot to garner a little extra power. Both methods work, so experiment to see which is best for you.

Begin with both knees slightly bent. The front leg moves first, either by scooting the lead foot forward a few inches, or by pivoting on the ball of the foot. The rear heel starts out flat but comes up as it drives your energy forward. At the conclusion of the punch, the front leg will be nearly straightened.

Many fighters use foot movement, finding that it adds weight to the punch and helps to turn the waist and hips. Others find they don't need to use the feet because they can generate enough force with precision body mechanics.

Whether you use this slight foot movement depends on

From the setup position, explode with a snap of the wrist, twist of the waist, contraction of the abdominals, and a slight scoot of the feet.

your needs, but the steps that follow are necessary to maximize your power.

Extend your arm, placing the middle knuckle of your index finger against the can, fist angled down slightly. Your forearm is parallel with the floor, and the knob of your elbow points down. Deliver the punch by snapping, or rocking the hand up so that you make contact with the knuckles of your little, ring, and middle fingers. Be sure your elbow is still pointing down at impact.

As your fist snaps up, execute a sharp twist of your waist. Contract your abdomen muscles as intensely as you can and mentally thrust all your energy, all your physical and mental power (refer to Chapter 1, "Ki Power") forward in one explosive movement. Think of striking two inches through the target.

Immediately recoil your hand after impact. This is a snapping blow, not a push. The target, whether it's the coffee can or your training partner's hand-held pad, should be knocked back with a shocklike impact.

Use Your Startle Reflex

The explosive movement needed to deliver the one-inch punch is rather like a startle reflex. Imagine that you are moving down a hallway in the dark, looking for the source of a mysterious noise. You move slowly, stealthily, your breathing shallow, your nerves taut. As you step in front of a doorway a dark figure emerges.

It's that startle, that heart-slamming, breath-catching, muscle-tensing, adrenaline-rushing moment that you want to capture in your explosive thrust.

Don't Push

This is not a push, though all too many times fighters make it one as a result of improper execution. The most common error is for the puncher to overextend his arm and fail to recoil his fist. When that is the case and the target is someone's chest, the person is knocked backward—but just knocked backward. But when the technique is executed with shock, the person still gets knocked backward, but he also experiences a wave of pain, perhaps severe trauma at the point of impact.

The upward snap of the wrist must explode like a gunshot. It's believed that mastery of the wrist snap alone can double the acceleration of the body's mass at the point of impact. It's important that you develop strong wrists and forearms to maximize snapping power.

How to Hold the Striking Pad

Once you have learned the proper execution of the one-inch punch, you will be able to deliver a blow powerful enough to hurt your training partner if he isn't holding the striking pad properly. The pad should never be held over the solar plexus or the heart. Even though the pad will absorb most of the force, it's still possible to transfer enough energy to cause injury to the holder.

The pad should be held *against* the upper chest, not an inch or two away so that the struck pad gets slammed against the holder's chest. The holder should be relaxed so that he can either roll with the punch or let the impact knock him backward. If the holder stiffens his body and tries to resist the force, he will absorb the impact and may be injured.

Is the One-Inch Punch Practical?

Opportunities to use the one-inch punch are rare because the position of your body has to be precise and all your body parts must come together in one perfectly synchronized move. If there is an opportunity, however, there is little doubt that it will cause severe injury.

You will not develop explosive power in the one-inch punch overnight; it will take time and effort. In the end, you will have learned how to coordinate your entire body to bring forth an extraordinary amount of power in a seemingly effortless movement. The knowledge and skill you gain from the practice will overlap to other techniques.

CHAPTER THIRTEEN

BAG WORK

There was a study conducted once in which several karate students were split into three groups. One group practiced their techniques only in the air, the second group practiced only on heavy bags, and the third group practiced half the time in the air and half on heavy bags. In the end, members of the first group, who practiced only in the air, improved their speed but were weak when they struck the bag. The second group developed power on the bags but lacked speed when punching and kicking the air. The third group improved both its speed in the air and power on the heavy bag. The moral of the story is don't ignore your bag work.

Let's look at how you can use bags to develop your hitting power.

KICKING SHIELDS

When you buy your first kicking shield, get a thick one. One of my students, who possesses extremely powerful kicks, once slammed a kick into a lightweight shield and broke the shield holder's thumb. Your power is going to increase quickly, so don't waste your time and money on a shield that in a few months isn't going to be big enough to handle your kicks.

A nice advantage of a kicking shield is that it's light and mobile, so the holder can move around and give you a variety of kicking situations. You will find that a mobile target is more difficult to hit with power than a stationary one.

As with any bag, the kicking shield allows you to unleash everything you have, as opposed to kicking the air where you consciously or unconsciously hold back. How you practice is how you will do in a real situation. Hard, full-contact kicking into a shield, or into any type of bag, will condition your mind and body for kicking full power.

The side benefit of this is that by practicing repeatedly against a shield, you learn how to properly unleash your kicking power. Although your instructor teaches you correct body mechanics, only through repetition will you discover the little nuances necessary to unleash your body's maximum kicking power.

To develop accuracy, place an X in the center of the kicking shield so that you can focus on a small point. But if you think only of kicking *at* the X, your foot will stop where your mind stops. For maximum power, you must think and kick into the shield at least six inches.

There are many kicking drills you can do against shields, and you can use just about any kick you want. One way to build power quickly is to double up on your kicks—that is, instead of kicking once, kick twice or even three times. Try these two methods.

Double Tap

Many police departments train their officers to always shoot twice, *double tapping* they call it. Let's try this principle with the kicking shield.

Your training partner holds the bag in anticipation of your roundhouse kicks. You can use either the front or rear leg to whip a hard kick into the shield, retract it, bounce it off the floor, and kick once again into the shield. The tendency when double kicking is for the second kick to be less powerful than the first. This is more a result of mentally relaxing than any physical limitation. Concentrate on the combination and push yourself to make that second kick as strong as, or stronger than, the first.

Repeat this same exercise with front, side, hook, and back kicks. You can either bounce the kick off the floor or retract it to the chambered position and launch the second one from there. Since it doesn't have as much momentum as the first kick, you have to rely on muscle power and hip rotation to drive it into the bag. Do 10 to 20 kicks with each leg.

Two Kicking Shields

You need two training partners with kicking shields for this exercise. Have one partner stand in front and one to your rear. Choose two kicks, say the front kick and back kick. From your fighting stance, drive a hard front kick into the front shield, retract your leg, and kick straight back into the rear shield. You can touch the floor in between or shoot the second one straight back without touching it.

You are limited by your imagination as to what configuration to use in this exercise. You can position the kicking shields diagonally right or left to your front, 90 degrees to the left or right, or diagonally to your rear.

This is a great exercise because it works two sets of major kicking muscles in the same drill. Push yourself to hit both bags as hard as you can for 10 to 20 kicks with each leg.

To work the front kick muscles, kick forward into the shield and then kick the rear shield to strengthen the back kick muscles.

THE HEAVY BAG

A friend of mine, Bill, who stands six-foot-six and weighs a hard 230, has trained in a number of martial art systems for many years and is so strong he could punch the grill out of a Ford pickup. While training with a kung fu class in China, Bill stopped to watch an old, frail-looking man punch a heavy bag. With each punch by the old man, the bag would fly through the air, threatening the chain that held it to the rafters. After several minutes, he stepped aside and gestured for my friend to give it a shot.

Bill stepped in front of the bag and prepared himself to smash it in a way that would show the class what American power was all about. With an exhalation of air, he slammed the bag with his best punch. His hand has never been the same since.

The bag was hard as stone. Not only did it not move, but all of Bill's energy went right back into his wrist, injuring it so badly that it still bothers him today. The old man just laughed at my friend's embarrassment and pain and resumed punching away as before, sending the bag flipping and flopping through the air.

Though many martial artists develop impressive knuckles from punching the rough exterior of a heavy bag, the bag's primary purpose is to develop power and to get you accustomed to the feel of hitting a heavy, yet absorbent target. The shock to the joints helps you condition yourself for hitting objects that transfer energy back. Punching the air does not give you this feeling. The bag is like a mirror: it won't lie to you. When you slam a hard punch into it, the shock from the blow passes through your wrist, elbow, shoulder, neck, upper body, hips, and down to your legs. If you are holding your hand or foot incorrectly and you blast it with a powerful blow, the bag will reflect your error by punishing you with excruciating pain. It will correct your errors by forcing you to consciously or subconsciously make the right adjustments until you are able to hit with full mastery. It's at this point that you will begin to increase your power.

Training on the heavy bag must be systematic. You will not make gains if you only punch or kick the bag once a month or every two weeks. Just as with your weight-training schedule, you need to work the heavy bag at least twice a week, scheduling it so that there are about 48 hours between sessions to allow your fatigued muscles to recover.

If you are able, get a lightweight bag, say 50 to 60 pounds, and a heavy one, 100 to 120 pounds. If you have access to only one heavy bag, you will have to make do. If you are new at heavy-bag training, or if you have an injury, start out on the light bag and stay with it for a month or so until you think your joints and muscles can handle the harder impact. If you are nursing an injury, let your pain or your doctor be your guide.

Start Out Slow

Start out hitting the bag with all of your punches and kicks. Use the lighter bag at first, or if you only have a heavy one, hit it with light to medium blows.

Do not omit techniques from heavy-bag training, such as the ridge hand, or that flippy-dippy kick you always score with in point-karate tournaments. If you don't do a technique on the heavy bag, how do you know the technique can withstand hard impact, and how do you know how hard you can hit with it?

Take the time to work on the heavy bag with all your techniques so that you know and understand them. It takes time to work out the nuances that allow you to hit with full power. If you try to progress too quickly and start working on combinations too soon, you run the risk of hurting yourself or unconsciously learning to hit with reduced power.

Time to Move Up

Once you feel comfortable hitting the lighter bag with hard blows, it's time to advance to the heavier one; or if you only have one bag, it's time to really start slamming it. Your power will increase rapidly, and your stamina will improve because 15 minutes of bag work accelerates the heart rate as much as running sprints. You will also develop distance perception, footwork, and timing.

Now is the time to put together your combinations, pushing yourself to hit harder and harder. Know that if you always hit at the same intensity, you won't grow. Only by pushing yourself mentally and physically will your power increase.

Establish your own style of hitting. It may be the same one used by your training buddies, or it may be unique to you. It doesn't matter; what's important is that you are using the correct body mechanics that bring out your maximum power.

Ranges

Explore techniques in the three ranges on the bag: close, middle, and long. At close range, hit with your head, elbows, knees, shoulders, hips, and chest. At middle range, use your punches, strikes, backfists, hammer blows, chops, and uppercuts. At long range, use all of your kicks—the basic ones for sure and any fancy ones you want to work on.

Experiment with combining the ranges. For example, hit the bag with a roundhouse kick, set your foot down in front and throw a reverse punch, and hit with an elbow. You can then reverse the direction by starting in close with an elbow strike, moving back and reverse punching in middle range, and then moving out to long range and throwing a roundhouse kick. Work this combination until you can hit hard in all three ranges. Strive for smooth transitions from blow to blow, making sure to use all the correct body mechanics to bring out your maximum power potential.

Footwork

You used linear footwork when you worked ranges in the last section, but you can also move around the bag in a circle, diagonally, sideways, zigzag, or any other way you want. Use your favorite footwork in combination with your kicks and punches. If your footwork is preventing you from hitting with power, figure out why. No doubt the problem is one of body mechanics, so you will need to take the time to correct the problem. If you can't, consider discarding the footwork, at least for that particular technique. Strive to make your footwork and combinations efficient, fluid, fast, and powerful.

Even though another fighter may make a combination look great, it may not work for you. Create combinations that use techniques that fit your body type and skill level.

Drive yourself. Remember, your goal is to gain greater power, and you won't get it training in a rut. You have to push yourself to improve. Do each single repetition and each combination a minimum of 20 times. Beginners and intermediate fighters should start out hitting medium hard and gradually increase the power of their blows until they are blasting away at full power. If you are advanced and have complete confidence in your techniques, go ahead and do all of your reps full power after you warm up.

If you spend 20 to 30 minutes on the heavy bag twice a week, you will see a definite improvement in two months. Your cardiovascular system will improve, and your techniques will hit with power in all three ranges.

Plyometric Heavy-Bag Pushing

This is a unique approach to developing power in your punches—and you don't even have to hit the bag. As in all plyometric exercises, this one emphasizes explosiveness of movement.

Stand with your left leg forward, arms up in a fighting stance, and push the heavy bag away with both hands. When it returns, absorb its force with both hands (your arms will be forced back a few inches) and then push it away quickly and forcefully. You want to catch it just after it passes through the vertical position so that its force is absorbed during its greatest momentum. Don't throw your body against it; use the muscles of your arms, shoulders, chest, and back to thrust it away violently. Do three sets of 10 reps and alternate left foot and right-foot-forward stances.

Plyometric Heavy-Bag Hitting

In this somewhat tricky variation, you will hit the bag but not until an instant after your fist makes contact with it. In other words, you won't be reaching out to strike the bag's surface as you normally do, but rather waiting until it passes the vertical line. Then when it makes contact with your fist, explode into it mentally and physically.

If your hands make a loud smack when you hit the bag, you are hitting too soon and doing the exercise no differently than when you normally hit it. To make the exercise plyometric, you need to absorb a little of the bag's momentum to stretch the muscles and then explode your energy back into it. The hit is actually occurring after your fists are already in contact with the bag. Do three sets of 10 reps.

Plyometric Push Kicks

Assume a left-leg-forward stance and push the heavy bag away from you. As it swings back, stop it with your foot just after it passes through the vertical, and then instantly and explosively push it away. What makes this exercise plyometric is that your leg muscles will get a stretch from the bag's weight and momentum before you push it.

Punching the Bag While Holding Weights

Bruce Lee recommended this method of heavy-hand hitting for people who were unable, for whatever reason, to learn how to use their ki. Although he believed ki power to be more powerful, he thought the following exercise came close to developing the same force.

Obtain a metal cylinder that weighs three to four pounds. It can't be too large because the large diameter will cause you to make an improper fist. Hold it lightly in your punching hand and throw a reverse punch at the heavy bag.

Maintain the light grip right up to the point of impact and then squeeze the cylinder just as your fist makes contact.

By holding the weight, you will notice a greater sense of power in your blows and a feeling of deeper penetration. Concentrate on hitting past the surface of the bag at least a couple of inches. Even when you think you have hit as deeply as you can, strive to extend an inch deeper. Make sure this is one, continuous motion rather than a two-part hit.

After you have punched with the weight for a while, strike the bag a few times without it. Doesn't feel quite as powerful, does it? Grab the weight again and punch the bag a few more times, being cognizant of feeling the weight and the difference it makes when you hit. Now hit the bag again without it, but imagine that you still have it in your hands and remember how it feels. In time, you will begin to hit the bag as if you are holding the weight. Your mind is most important in this exercise. You must be focused on the task at hand.

CHAPTER FOURTEEN

POWER THROUGH TIMING

I think there is nothing more beautiful than a perfectly timed punch or kick. Precise timing defines the art—call it perfection through movement. As discussed in *Speed Training*, perfect timing will make a slow fighter fast and a moderately strong person powerful.

When body positioning, if you combine momentum, surprise, gravity, and other elements with precise timing, the power of your punch or kick will be greatly increased. Combine this with what you develop from all of the exercises in this book and your techniques will be more powerful than you ever imagined.

Let's take a brief look at a few perfectly timed techniques that will add power to your blows.

SIMULTANEOUS BLOCK AND COUNTER

This works best when the attacker is moving toward you. For example, as the attacker charges in with a hard reverse punch, step off slightly to one side, snap out a block, and drive a punch of your own into the attacker's chest. Your block and counter must occur simultaneously in one fluid motion. Your attacker's forward momentum will add power to your blow, and he will be plenty surprised at getting hit just as he thought his blow was going to land.

MOMENTUM MEETS MOMENTUM

In this case your opponent is lunging to kick or punch you. Just as he crosses that invisible line that puts him within your kicking range, drive a front kick into his middle.

You can also step diagonally forward as he comes into range so that his attack misses and then whip a roundhouse kick into him. This is not as powerful as an impaling kick, but it has the potential to knock him on his rear.

HITTING WHEN BOBBING AND WEAVING

Your timing has to be right on the money with

As the attacker lunges in with a jab, step off at an angle and slap his face using momentum and your arm strength to make the blow powerful.

this one or you will be dining on a handful of knuckles. When the attacker snaps out a jab, move your head and upper body to the right or left, just enough to avoid getting hit. For example, as you move to the right, drive home a left punch into his body, combining the speed of your punch with the momentum of your body and his. You can also hit

Bob your head away from the blow and whip a powerful forearm strike into the attacker's groin.

with your knee. Bob to the left when the attacker punches and drive your right knee into his middle. Again, you are taking advantage of your and your opponent's momentum to increase the power of your blow.

DRAWING

This doesn't work every time, but when it does, it works like a charm. As you and your partner are moving around stalking each other, take a sudden step backward. Half the time your opponent will follow you. When he does, burst forward with a punch or kick and nail him, again using the force of your forward momentum and his.

BREAK THE CIRCLE

This works well against an opponent who likes to stalk

you in a circle, either to the left or the right. Most of the time he isn't aware that he is moving in such a pattern, so go along with him for a few seconds and let him lock the circle into his mind. When the moment seems right, abruptly lunge into his path. Most of the time he will change direction, exactly what you want him to do. Here is what usually happens.

Say you step out at an angle in front of him but leave your rear foot trailing. His reaction will be to try to escape in the opposite direction, exactly where your foot is anxiously waiting. When he moves into range, whip a hard kick into his groin. Your body mechanics are not ideal, so the kick won't be your strongest, but you will get some help from your opponent's momentum.

CHAPTER FIFTEEN

DEFENDING AGAINST POWER

I f you have seen the movie *Gettysburg* or any of the many paintings to come out of the Civil War, you may have wondered why the troops stood virtually toe-to-toe and blasted away at each other. Why didn't they take cover or sidestep or do something to get out of the way of those big hairy bullets they used back then?

During the 1860s, standing in long lines across from each other and shooting was just the way they fought. It was the "code of the warrior" of those times.

Today, that code no longer exists. There are no rules that say you must stand toe-to-toe with your opponent and slug it out, a situation where the strongest, fastest, and most accurate will come out on top. However, there are styles that are primarily linear; that is, they are fought in a straight line, straight in, straight out. This is especially effective if you weigh 250 and can bench press 500 pounds, because there are few people bigger and stronger. But if you are of average size, moving straight in on an opponent who is your size or larger may not be in your best interest.

Keep in mind that you can't always determine how hard a fighter can hit by how he looks. There are many 160-pound fighters out there who can hit like a 200-pound guy (probably as a result of reading this book). As mentioned earlier, Bruce Lee weighed only 136 pounds but was said to hit harder than a man twice that weight.

You can't always tell by looking, so you shouldn't automatically assume you can fight a smaller fighter with less caution than you would a larger fighter. Making the assumption that you can simply wade in on a seemingly inferior opponent may get you reduced to a grease spot on the floor.

BLOCKING WITHOUT BLOCKING

One way to defend against power, no matter what the opponent's physical size, is to simply not be there when the power comes your way. If the grays and the blues would have tried this during the Civil War, there would have been far fewer casualties.

Bodyshifting

Bodyshifting is one way to avoid a powerful blow. Not only do you avoid getting hit, but you also avoid the potential of damaging your blocking limb. With some blocks, especially those that meet force head on, there is the potential of causing injury or temporary debilitation to the blocking limb and leaving it useless. Additionally, there are some fighters so powerful they can easily smash through your blocks.

When bodyshifting, you move or lean in any direction that best gets you out of the way but still positions you so that you can hit with a solid counter. Because you are not stopping your opponent's force when you bodyshift, your limbs remain healthy and your balance stays intact.

How far you move is important. If you shift too far away from the attacker and can't reach him with your counter, you have not advanced your situation. If you try and charge across the gap to execute your counter, you increase the chance of getting hit. You want to move away just enough to avoid the attack, but be close enough to instantly strike back to slow down or eliminate any follow-up that the attacker may have in mind.

Whether you are fighting in competition or in the street, the quality of the stance you shift into is important so that you can hit swiftly and with as much power as possible. It's necessary, therefore, to practice bodyshifting so that you incorporate maximum body mechanics into your movements. Bodyshifting sloppily is just as bad as trying to block a powerful attack and getting knocked off balance.

Moving Straight Back

Although there are times you should evade by moving

If you choose to evade a kick by backing up, be careful not to move so far that you are unable to counter.

back in a straight line, there are a couple of reasons why this should not become a habit.

Moving back when an opponent is charging forward can cause you to trip or lose your balance. Few people can back up fast and keep their feet under them for more than a few steps. Second, when backing away from an aggressor, it's common to go too far out of range and not be able to counterattack. You may avoid the attack, but you end up back where you began.

A linear defense will work against a strong fighter who you know attacks only once or twice on a straight line and then stops in range. You move back only enough to avoid his charge and to counter with a blow to the closest target. But if you don't know whether he will stop after one or two charging blows, your best bet is to step off diagonally.

Moving Diagonally

Instead of moving straight back, it's better to step at an angle, forward or backward, to avoid the charge and position yourself to blast home a solid counterattack. This requires precise timing and distancing, and can only be accomplished through practice with a live partner. But first you must practice the mechanics of the movement by yourself.

Assume a fighting stance with your left leg forward. Take a step back diagonally with your right foot and draw your left leg back so that you are facing your invisible opponent at a slight angle. When your right leg is forward, simply reverse the directions. Repeat as many times on both sides as needed to develop smoothness and quickness.

Now do it with your partner. Have him launch a front kick at your midsection. Time it so that you move your rear leg back diagonally just enough to avoid the kick. If he sets his leg down in front, he will probably be close enough that you can counter with a hand technique. If he retracts his kick and sets it behind him, you may or may not be able to get him with a punch. If not, you will have to counter with a long-range kick. Practice until you can do it smoothly.

MISCELLANEOUS EVASIONS

Many of the same evasion techniques discussed and illustrated in *Speed Training* will work against a powerful attacker, such as body twisting, head evasion, and crowding.

Body Twisting

This involves twisting the upper body away from a push, punch, or kick attack. It can be done with or without footwork. If a push attack comes at you slightly off center to the right side of your chest, twist your upper body to the right. If there is time, shift your entire stance to evade even more.

Your objective is to twist away before the attacker touches you, but usually you will be a fraction of a second too late and the attacker will get a piece of you. But not all is lost. If you can still twist away a split second after the touch, you can dissipate the major portion of the attacker's power.

Twist your upper body sharply to the side to evade a push.

Head Evasion

The head is a small, mobile target and is relatively easy to move out of the path of a powerful blow. It can be moved to the right, left, back, or forward, and you can scrunch it down like a turtle withdrawing into its shell. All this can be done with or without moving the feet.

You should include neck flexibility exercises along with any resistance exercises you do. The resistance training will build strength in your neck, and the flexibility exercises will ensure that the muscles will move your head out of the way quickly and smoothly.

Crowding

There are times when crowding a strong fighter will take away his power. For example, let's say a powerful puncher swings a blow at your head. If other options are out of the question, move in quickly and attack with close-quarter techniques: elbows, knees, headbutts, and bites.

Your success depends on your ability to explode so fast and furiously that your opponent is overwhelmed and unable to use his powerful techniques.

If your big opponent absorbs your blows and begins striking back with his own, get out of range as quickly as you can, but don't stop hitting. Too many fighters make the mistake of moving out of close range, passing through middle range, and then long range. They are so concerned with escaping their opponent's blows they never hit back with their own. That approach will get you hurt. You must continue to throw blows as long as you are close enough to hit your opponent. Think of it this way: when you are not hitting, your opponent has the opportunity to hit you. Make it your personal rule that as long as you are close enough to hit, you will hit.

Evading Low Kicks

If the range between you and your opponent is just right, you can evade a low-level kick. For example, to evade a kick fired at your lead shin, simply raise your leg high enough to make the kicker miss.

You can also quickly switch your stance using a simple move I call a "poor man's Ali shuffle." Boxer Mohammed Ali used to do a thing he called the Ali shuffle, in which he would switch his feet back and forth several times to confuse his opponent. The move was always followed immediately by a solid punch to his opponent's chops.

When I do my version, it's done to both evade and create a forward momentum for my counter. When my opponent pops a front kick at my forward left knee, I quickly move my left foot back to my right foot, so that his kick misses and then move my right foot forward as I drive home a hard counterattack. Sometimes you will need to make the switch quickly, other times you may have to hold your position after your feet come together to wait for the attacker to retract his leg.

ARM AND HAND BLOCKING

A friend of mine is 6 foot 7 and weighs 270 pounds of weight-trained muscle. He has rock-hard abdominal muscles and arms the size of a steer. Over the years he has only dabbled in the martial arts, never remaining with one fighting art long enough to earn a belt. He studied with me for a few weeks and then had to quit for personal reasons. I remember vividly the times he swatted aside my punches and how my shoulders felt as if they were going to be dislocated.

The point is this: given this man's great size and incredible power, there is no way anyone can stop his punch, untrained as it is, by simply shielding oneself with raised forearms like a boxer. His bare fist would effortlessly smash through them like a giant boulder dropping through straw. I know, I tried.

So how can one deal with this kind of power?

Sweep Blocks

A sweep block does exactly as the name implies: it sweeps the attack aside. It doesn't deal with the force straight on, but simply moves it out of the way.

Assume your fighting stance, left side forward. As your opponent's straight punch comes straight in toward your chest, sweep it aside with a short, quick slap with your left open palm. There is no need to start the movement from way back, loading it up, so to speak, and there is no need to sweep past the edge of your body to the far right side. Your chest doesn't exist in those places, so don't waste the time and effort. Simply sweep the attack to the edge of your body and then deliver your counterattack.

The sweep works against all straight punches and uppercuts to the face, chest, and abdomen. Usually, your

A smaller fighter can defend against a powerful punch by simply sweeping the force aside.

sweep will make contact against your opponent's hand or wrist area, but if you want to give your attacker's arm a little shock, slap your sweep against his elbow joint.

You can also sweep in a diagonal direction. From the left-side-forward stance, sweep your left palm diagonally up to your right or diagonally down to your right. Your rear right hand can sweep up diagonally to your left or down diagonally.

By the way, sweep blocks worked like a charm against my big friend.

Rising Block

There are no absolutes in life and certainly not in fighting. Even though I highly recommend deflection blocks and evasive stepping, there are times when you have to block force with force. A powerful circular punch, such as a roundhouse, delivered at close range, is one such situation. When you are too close to evade or parry it, you have to meet force with force. Or as a staunch, hard-style traditionalist, you may deliberately meet force with force in an attempt to injure your attacker's limbs. Whatever the case, let's examine the characteristics of the rising block, one of the best for this situation, and see how it can be made effective against a powerful attack.

Hips. Yes, once again the ol' hips are all-important to add power to a technique. To use them in the rising block, you must snap your hips in the direction your blocking arm is moving and at the same time it's moving.

For example, stand in a left-leg-forward stance, your arms in their usual fighting position, your hips angled 45 degrees to your right. As your left arm snaps up into a rising block, snap the right hip forward to where your hips are square to the front. You may find the block to be faster and stronger if you lead with your arm and follow with the hip action, or you may prefer to move your arms and hips at the same time. Experiment to see which works best for you.

Combining hip rotation with the rising block also works well from most fighting stances. It won't work if your hips are straight on, as if facing your opponent in a horse stance—I can't imagine anyone fighting that way, anyway—and it's difficult to do when fighting from a side horse stance. It can be done, however, if your horse is at a 45-degree angle to your opponent.

Some fighters leave their block in place as they counter with either hand or foot, while other fighters use the snap-back method, similar to a snapping backfist. In either case, if you think of the hard rising block as a strike, you will increase the block's power dramatically.

When all the elements are added to the rising block— fast hip rotation, fast snap-back of the blocking hand, strong mental intent—your power will virtually double. In addition, if you train with weight-resistance exercises, dynamic tension, and free-hand exercises, your opponent will never again want to throw a roundhouse punch at you.

Leg Checking

Leg checking is an effective way to deflect a powerful kicker who likes to kick below the belt. By moving the force away from you, the attack dissipates into space and leaves you in a good position to counterattack.

Deflecting force with the leg works especially well against straight-in kicks: front, side, and straight back. Kicks such as roundhouse, crescent, and hook types are more difficult to deflect because of their circular direction of force.

You may use either leg for deflecting, though the front leg is usually faster because it's closer to the attack. The rear leg is generally used when your weight is on the front leg and there is insufficient time to switch.

You can either use the outside or the inside of the shin, depending on which is more efficient for the particular attack. For example, when your powerful opponent launches a side kick just left of your center as you stand with your left leg forward, it's more efficient to deflect the attack to the left with the outside of your lead leg. If you were to deflect it to the right, the chance of your getting nailed with the attack would be much greater since you would be sweeping the leg across your body. Experiment with this block against all straight kicks that come at you a little off center.

Strive to be cognizant that you are using the most efficient method of deflecting each attack. Granted, there may be times when you are successful with a less efficient block; luck may be with you once or twice, but you may not be as successful the next time. Always train to be as efficient as possible.

Blocking such circular kicks as roundhouse, hook, and crescent with your lower leg can be painful to your shin because you are meeting force with force. Whenever you absorb the full impact of a kick against your shin, it's generally because you have no choice, such as when an attack has tremendous speed or catches you by surprise. However, if you have enough warning that a powerful kick is en route to your legs or groin, you can dissipate some of its force by bodyshifting or side-stepping in the direction of the force.

Let's say your opponent throws a hard roundhouse kick at your left leg and the force is coming from your left to your right. You have enough warning that you can quickly take one step to the right, in the direction of the incoming force, and then lift your leg to check the slightly dissipated kick. Lean your body toward the force so that you won't get knocked over.

CHAPTER SIXTEEN

WHY ARE MY PUNCHES AND KICKS STILL WIMPY?

Y ou have been lifting weights, doing push-ups, and running up hills carrying buckets of rocks, but still your techniques lack power. Why is it that sometimes a smaller student can explode into a heavy bag like a cannonball, while some big guys hit with no more power than a little bunny?

I knew a nationally ranked karate fighter who told me that the spinning crescent kick was weak and ineffectual. I had to agree when he demonstrated his crescent. Then I had a student of mine—a man who weighs 160 pounds and can kick the bag with extraordinary power—demonstrate his crescent. When the champion saw my student's crescent, he quickly changed his mind about the kick and began working to improve his.

Why does this happen? Why do some people have

power, while others who train hard and look powerful don't? Why, after all the sweat and blood you have shed, does power still elude you?

Let's take a look at the most common problems that affect power. All of these things are discussed throughout this book, so use the following as a troubleshooter checklist to consider remedies.

GENERAL OR SPECIFIC LACK OF POWER

By now, you have been training in your fighting art for months, and though you are using correct body mechanics, your techniques still lack power. Assuming that your general health is good and you are not overtraining, you need to supplement your training with specific power-developing exercises.

Use the information throughout this book to choose one exercise for each basic technique, such as one for punching, one for the backfist, and one for your front, round, and back kick. Do these twice a week on days when you don't train in your art. Change each exercise once a month and don't overtrain. Eat healthily, get plenty of rest, and expect to see an overall improvement in your power in three to four months.

Let's say your general power is progressing nicely but that your front kick still lacks power. Choose one exercise from the following list, two if you are advanced and in shape:

- Weightless squats
- High jumps
- Weighted squats
- High-rep kicking
- Leg extensions
- Horse stance exercises
- Slow front kicks
- Heavy-bag kicking

Create your own specialized program and work at it diligently. You will start seeing a difference in about three months, but that doesn't mean you stop training once you have become stronger. Strength is fleeting; if you don't work at it, it's going to dissipate.

And don't forget proper eating habits. You can't develop power on potato chips and hamburgers.

LACK OF SPEED

If you have evaluated all the elements in this troubleshooter checklist and made corrections but still lack speed, you need to work on specific elements, such as reflex speed, perception speed, movement speed, timing, and various ways of creating the illusion of being fast.

Boy, do I have a super, wonderful, fantastic book for you! Order a copy of *Speed Training* by yours truly, available through Paladin Press. It contains a variety of exercises and drills designed to bring out your maximum speed.

Here is a fun thing to think about. Besides physically training for speed, you can actually gain speed by thinking yourself faster. There is nothing mystical about this, but rather a conviction in your own mind that you possess fast techniques. I happily discovered in the course of writing *Speed Training* that I was becoming faster simply because I was thinking about it so much. Many experts on speed training teach that if you believe you are fast, you will be fast. Try it.

TIMING

Precise timing will not only enhance your speed, or at least create the illusion of it, but it will create additional power. If your timing is off, your techniques will miss the target or be fully extended, which is the same thing as missing. When your timing is on, your blow will hit at the precise moment your opponent is open and the instant he is within range.

The best way to develop timing is to practice against moving targets, such as moving hand pads, a swinging heavy bag, various moving objects, and sparring partners. Sparring partners are the best because they are the most erratic and the most unpredictable. And the larger the variety of partners you can train with, the better off you will be.

When you spar to improve timing, it's important to pay attention to what is going on. You are not competing with your partner, but rather learning from him. If you continually engage in one-upmanship, you are not going to learn as quickly from your successes and errors.

Approach your sparring analytically. If one of your punches or kicks gets in, stop and analyze why. If you consistently miss with a kick or punch, stop and analyze why. Have your sparring partner repeat whatever he was doing just before you made your attempt. Is he too far away? Too close? Are you telegraphing your intention? To analyze what worked for you, have him repeat what he was doing when you hit him successfully. Ask your partner his opinion on what you are doing wrong and what you are doing right.

Too often when students spar, they are not learning; in fact, they often end up reinforcing bad habits. To learn, make sure you include analytical sparring in your training and watch your power improve.

LACK OF CONCENTRATION

It's rather difficult to deliver a powerful blow if you miss the opportunity to throw it. Obviously, you have got to be mentally into your training, your competition, and your fight if you are going to have success. It's not always easy, however, especially given the hectic schedules so many people have today.

It's important to "shut off your day" before you start training. You want an uncluttered mind, free to respond to whatever comes your way. It won't happen if you are angry about what your boss said to you that morning or if you are worried about a math test the next day.

When I was studying t'ai chi a few years ago, I would arrive early and relax in my car for 10 minutes before going in. I would scoot down in the seat, close my eyes, and practice slow, deep breathing. I would concentrate on the cool air flooding my body, soothing my tension, relaxing my muscles, and calming my mind. This simple procedure made me alert and receptive to the lessons. On those days I was late and unable to have this little moment, my lesson suffered.

Many martial art schools begin their classes with a few minutes of meditation. If your school does this, take advantage of these moments to clear your mind of the day's clutter and prepare yourself for training.

Actually, you don't have to wait until just moments before your training to prepare your mind. You can start from your first waking moment by telling yourself that you will not let the many daily irritations get the best of you. Granted, this is easier said than done, and it's beyond the scope of this book to tell you the intricacies of how to do it. But if gathering stress throughout the day is causing distractions in your training, it's worth the effort to research ways to deal with it. There are plenty of good self-help books on the market that address this problem, and many community colleges offer stress-reduction classes.

FLEXIBILITY

When your muscles are tight, you can't hit hard. No matter how strong your legs are, your muscles need to be flexible enough to deliver your power smoothly and quickly. A muscle that lacks flexibility is a muscle that is being restrained.

Stretching exercises are often overlooked by the younger martial artist and by some people who simply think they don't need to do them. But it's absolutely mandatory to work on your flexibility, at least three times a week.

A STIFF BODY

This is different from a lack of flexibility. Stiffness of movement is most often seen in new students for any number of reasons: poor physical condition, stress, nervousness, and excessive muscle flexing. This usually occurs because they have entered a new world and are uncertain about what to expect. Time usually takes care of this problem, although the process can be accelerated by practicing breathing and relaxation exercises.

Some new students have a tendency to flex or tense their muscles as they practice, usually because they believe they have to flex and strain in order to get power in their techniques. Not true. In fact, the more a muscle is flexed, the slower and weaker it will be.

Physical conditioning will eventually improve as you train and develop your muscles and cardiovascular system. Approach your conditioning sensibly—be cautious about doing too much—follow a healthy diet and get plenty of rest.

TRYING TOO HARD

This can happen to veterans as well as new students, and it's commonly seen in real fights. In an effort to throw a hard kick or a powerful punch, the student throws everything into it: body weight, balance, and stability, causing the attacker to lose his balance and fall down.

Time and training will often take care of this problem, as the student's skill level increases and he begins to understand how much energy to put into a technique. He will learn that with control of his body (that is, mastery of the particular body mechanics involved in a technique) he will generate the power he wants.

Fear and stress can cause a fighter to put too much

into a technique. As your confidence develops along with your skill, you will gain greater control of your body and emotions. Continual work on relaxation and stress reduction will help you gain better control of the energy you apply to a technique.

• • •

Never accept a problem. Although that sounds like a logical statement, there are many students who simply accept as gospel that they are slow, weak, clumsy, or whatever. Seek out a solution to your training problems. That is part of what the martial arts are all about—self-discovery. Discuss the problem with a teacher or an advanced student, or research the tons of literature in the library and in bookstores. Strive to be the best that you can be.

CHAPTER SEVENTEEN

BITS OF WISDOM

H ere are a few bits of wisdom on developing power that I have picked up over the years in the martial arts, as well as in researching this book. Don't just glance over them and forget them. Those that appear the most simplistic may be the most complex. Read them, think about them, and incorporate them into your training.

- To deliver maximum kicking power, lean back slightly and kick with your entire body rather than just your legs.
- Choose a school where the students exhibit powerful techniques.
- The faster you kick or punch, the greater your penetration will be.

- Set goals. When you reach one, set another. Your power will not increase if you maintain the status quo.
- When you kick, mentally project all of your body mass into the target.
- You are only in your school two or three times a week. You need to spend extra time away from the school working on supplemental power exercises.
- For maximum power, retract your opposite hand faster and harder than your punching hand.
- No matter how fast you are, if you don't have physical strength, you will not hit as hard as a fighter who is strong *and* fast.
- Practice with all your power and speed in your block and counter drills.
- If you practice your kata as if it is a matter of life or death, your speed and power will increase.
- Training should be consistent. You won't gain strength training irregularly.
- Powerful kicks require flexibility in addition to speed and strength.
- You can't hit hard if you don't hit fast.
- High kicks are not efficient because they require more energy and time than low kicks.
- Train to evade powerful low kicks and save your arms.
- When throwing a reverse punch, make sure your arm travels out in a straight line. If your elbow flips out to the side, you will lose power.
- Create mass by stepping into a blow.
- Believe that you have power. Self-confidence will increase your strength.
- Protective hand gear may create a weak fist. Punch the heavy bag from time to time without the gloves to ensure that you are making a tight fist and hitting with your two large knuckles.
- Instantly retracting your blow after impact can create internal injury to your opponent.
- Front snap kicks get their power from a snap of the knee

joint and a fast contraction of the hamstring muscles.
- Spin kicks get their power from the hips.
- Concentrate fully on the target.
- Do exercises to strengthen your wrists so that they don't bend when punching the heavy bag.
- Speed and power come from relaxation.
- Practice to put your body weight into knee strikes.
- Throwing reverse punches in neck-high water provides good resistance and lets you feel your errors.
- Strong abdominals mean stronger punches and kicks.
- You don't need a lot of expensive equipment to develop flexibility.
- A loud shout adds psychological and physical power to your techniques.
- Use your shin to block powerful low kicks.
- Hold dumbbells in your hands when practicing the horse stance.
- Hold your horse stance for five minutes to develop mental toughness.
- Do not prematurely tense your muscles when punching and kicking.
- If you consistently look down when you punch, you will cause your head to dip forward as well as your shoulders. This throws your body out of alignment and weakens your technique.
- Torque involves twisting the hips, shoulders, and fist. All contribute to greater power.
- Always hit with penetration.
- Never use power needlessly.
- When bench pressing, visualize that you are pushing someone off you.
- Squat deep enough in your horse stance so that you can lay a pole across your thighs without its rolling off.
- Practice shadow boxing in neck-high water to add resistance to your blows.
- Always get enough rest. You can't develop power if you are tired.

- You will never develop power if you lay off training every time you get injured. If you hurt your foot, do punches. If you hurt your hand, practice kicking.
- Always do power exercises at the conclusion of your training session or on off days.
- You will not develop power by eating junk food.
- Practice to ensure that speed accompanies your power.
- Warm up thoroughly before you train for power.

CONCLUSION

I have written at length in other Paladin books about my experiences as a military policeman in Vietnam and as a patrol officer in Portland, Oregon. To reiterate briefly, when I began using my training on the street, I quickly discovered that the streets are not the place for weak and flashy techniques. Those flippy-dippy kicks have no effect on a six-foot, 200-pound drunk bent on crumpling your face like a sheet of paper. Those back-fists and roundhouse kicks you are so convinced will knock down a building oftentimes are only an irritant to a street thug.

There are a lot of fighters who are fooling themselves. They train to deliver snappy punches and kicks with flare and finesse. They feel good about how the techniques look and how their uniforms crack with each strike. Unfortunately, they find out too late that these qualities don't help them on the street.

It would never happen to you, you say? Well, there have been many documented cases of black belts who thought the same thing, that is, until they woke up in a hospital.

There are three attributes that help you in a in real fight: surprise, speed, and power. Hit them before they know it, hit them several times, and hit them hard. Why would you do otherwise? If you have the right to defend yourself and the situation calls for you to use force, do it fast, do it hard, and end the situation before the attacker gets lucky.

My philosophy on training is that if you are going to take the time to do it, do it right. What so often happens among martial arts students is that they start out training for self-defense, but after a few months, that original premise gets put on the back burner as they get absorbed in learning the intricacies of the art. They may be learning fighting techniques, but the effort of learning the mechanics of movement, fulfilling belt requirements, and preparing for tournament competition dominates their minds.

As martial artists, we cannot lose the original premise of what the martial arts were originally created to do. Study for competition if you want, study for art's sake, and study for personal achievement. But take it from a guy who has come face to face with some pretty scary individuals, always keep in the forefront of your mind that someday you may need to fight for your life.

With that thought, you must strive to make your techniques fast enough and powerful enough to get the job done. If you are naturally fast and strong, don't accept that as sufficient. Never be satisfied. Push yourself to be the best you are capable of. Realize that you can always be faster and more powerful next week. But you have to keep training to get there.

ABOUT THE AUTHOR

Loren Christensen began studying the martial arts in 1965. He holds black belts in jujitsu and arnis and a seventh-degree black belt in karate. As a teacher, Loren is known for his pragmatic approach to the martial arts and is sought by police officers, mental health workers, school security officers, jail guards, and citizens who want to learn and practice realistic street-fighting techniques.

"The mean streets are no place for weak, flashy, flippy-dippy techniques, " he says. "Keep them simple but deliver them with awesome power and laserlike speed."